aboriginal rights are not human rights

Aboriginal Rights Are Not Human Rights

IN DEFENCE OF INDIGENOUS STRUGGLES

Peter Kulchyski

ARP BOOKS • WINNIPEG

Copyright ©2013 Peter Kulchyski

ARP Books (Arbeiter Ring Publishing)
201E-121 Osborne Street
Winnipeg, Manitoba
Canada R3L 1Y4
www.arpbooks.org

Printed in Canada by Kromar Printing
Cover by Michael Carroll
Typeset by Relish New Brand Experience

ARP acknowledges the financial support of our publishing activities by Manitoba Culture, Heritage, and Tourism, and the Government of Canada through the Canada Book Fund.

ARP acknowledges the support of the Province of Manitoba through the Book Publishing Tax Credit and the Book Publisher Marketing Assistance Program.

We acknowledge the support of the Canada Council for our publishing program.

With the generous support of the Manitoba Arts Council.

Printed on paper from 100% recycled post-consumer waste.

LIBRARY AND ARCHIVES CANADA CATALOGUING IN PUBLICATION

Kulchyski, Peter Keith, 1959-
     Aboriginal rights are not human rights : in defence of indigenous struggles / Peter Kulchyski.

(Semaphore series)
Includes bibliographical references.
ISBN 978-1-894037-76-1

     1. Native peoples--Legal status, laws, etc.--Canada. 2. Native peoples--Canada--Politics and government. 3. Native peoples--Canada--Social life and customs. I. Title. II. Series: Semaphore series

E78.C2K84 2013   971.004'97   C2013-901686-4

contents

foreword: letters from the trenches

a few years ago, allies of defenders of the land, a new indigenous activist organization in canada, engaged in an online debate about a document called our "basis of solidarity." i had paid passing attention to the debate, preoccupied with other concerns and with helping establish the organization's basic capacity. late in the increasingly sharp online debate, i decided to review the draft. i noted that the words "aboriginal rights" had disappeared, in spite of the fact that our indigenous leaders were committed to them, and inquired why the concept had been dropped. i then learned that a large sector of the social justice activist community was opposed to the idea of rights. in the wake of a united states-sponsored invasion of iraq ostensibly in the name of "freedom" and "democracy," many activists began seeing rights as a justification for state or imperial interventions rather than as a tool for marginalized

munities. i intervened in the debate through a lengthy
in academic standards quite schematic) email as
ws:

'm going to write a paragraph on indigenous rights
here, because i hadn't realized the issue was quite so
controversial in our groups. so you can skip this if you
haven't time, etc. the notion of rights is not liberal or
capitalist. it comes in the western tradition as far back
as the plebeians of rome/greece trying to wrest power
from the aristocrats, and from poorer people in a variety of situations around the world using the same idea,
often as a way of limiting the unrestrained power of the
rich. it's fair to say that the rich have also promoted a
notion of rights, property rights, and that this too goes
back a long way. the notion of rights became individualist in western europe from around the enlightenment.
possessive individualism became a core foundation of
capitalist legal frameworks, and it is still with us today.
the united nations declaration of human rights, and
the many other similar declarations, tend to be univer-
salistic, eurocentric, and individualist, though it still
has value as an obstacle to unimpeded capitalist development in certain contexts. neoliberalism is indeed
associated with an individualist property rights agenda.
aboriginal rights have an entirely different origin. they
come from the struggle of indigenous peoples to have
their customary practices and land ownership respected. they were not enshrined by the united nations
until decades after the universal declaration. they are by

nature collective (though they can be and most often are invoked by individuals on behalf of the collective: roberta keesig's fight to build a cabin was a fight for all anishinabe). if we truly respected indigenous rights we would be putting up a major, perhaps fatal, obstacle to neoliberal capitalist development. hence, i have no hesitation about my unqualified support for indigenous rights at the same time as having some serious questions about so called "universal" human rights (which need and sometimes do include a right of association) and absolutely despise possessive individual property rights. (22 october 2009)

the language of aboriginal rights was eventually maintained and strengthened in the "basis of unity" and other statements (see www.defendersoftheland.org). but the debate helped me realize that there are many well motivated people who have little understanding of the specific nature of aboriginal rights; in general, they tie the idea quite closely to broader notions of human rights, which, for a variety of legitimate ethical-political reasons, they have come to be suspicious of. it was this event and discussion that prompted me to write these words.

the confusion concerning differing conceptions of rights can be found in the analysis by close observers of the processes that led to the united nations' adoption of the declaration on the rights of indigenous peoples, and it can also be found in the declaration itself. in the chapters that follow, i discuss briefly and schematically the varying histories of human rights and aboriginal rights, demonstrate how the conceptual confusion between them operates to undermine aboriginal rights, lay out a structure for clarifying the problem, and show how the issue relates to some recent indigenous struggles in canada. indeed, much of what follows can be taken as reports from the battleground of aboriginal rights in canada, complete with tactical recommendations. throughout the book, i use the terms "indigenous" or "aboriginal" to describe the variety of peoples with whom the united nations declaration and my analyses are concerned. i use the term "aboriginal rights" to discuss the specific rights of indigenous peoples, and "indigenous human rights" to describe the human rights of indigenous peoples. the "rights of indigenous peoples" is a term used by the united nations that encompasses, for better or worse, both forms of rights.

if there is a "battleground" of aboriginal rights, where are the front lines? are the front lines the blockades and occupations that indigenous people establish at grassy narrows or grand rapids or in other even more well known locations? these are the sites that sometimes generate media attention and are the places where the struggles are condensed and intensified, where the often dormant issues suddenly demand confrontation. or are the front lines to be found deep in the bush, far from prying eyes and media attention, where aboriginal culture is enacted in practice? certainly these are places and moments that seem to put the broader struggle into something like perspective, though perhaps only a handful of the political agents ever get there. is the courtroom, a place where both the explicit political confrontations and the implicit politics of the cultural/daily activities that take place in the bush are adjudicated, the "proper" front line? the legal confrontations are, beyond a doubt, a place where practices and policies can be codified, boundaries drawn, principles of engagement established. perhaps the front lines are in our cities; for example, in the urban shaman gallery in winnipeg or in any of the many friendship centres that figure in so many urban spaces. the front lines could just as easily be in the history, politics, anthropology, literature, sociology, and law textbooks that define who is who and what happened to whom in whose interests. maybe the most real front line is the one inside each of us, that place where we keep our latent, lingering ability to care about each other, to care enough to try to understand, to care enough to act: this might be the most critical front line of all.

these letters from the trenches engage each of these front lines: sites of intense material struggle, legal debates, battles around images and ideologies propagated in a variety of disciplinary texts, urban actions, and political mobilizations, attempts to cajole and persuade, to remind people that there is a truer justice than that spoken by bureaucrats, a justice that cannot be separated from the poetry inherent in its making.

this book emerged from a series of articles that i published in *canadian dimension, new socialist,* and *briarpatch* magazines, as well as a couple of academic texts from the *journal of canadian studies* and *prairie forum.* it is based on essays originally written to help achieve specific political goals: to raise questions about the united nations declaration on the rights of indigenous peoples, for example, in the moment of its being triumphantly celebrated, or to displace the concept of class with the concept of mode of production in a socialist or materialist approach to indigenous politics. in fact, my main point and broadest theme is that for a socialist practice, the tool "mode of production" allows theoretical purchase onto the cultural value of indigenous hunting peoples. this in turn allows us to develop a properly socialist rationale for the concept of aboriginal rights. aboriginal rights belong within historical materialist theory and socialist practice, but must be sharply distinguished from human rights if that is to be the case. although primarily oriented to serve these theoretical and polemical purposes, the book also engages in reporting, using the issues created by manitoba hydro's assault on cree lands in northern manitoba or the meeting of a national network of activists—the defenders of the land—sometimes to make points, sometimes as events that fly below the mainstream media radar but deserve attention on the part of those who still retain a conscience.

my earlier book, *the red indians*, roughly acts as a brief introduction to aboriginal history in canada, written for those with a social justice and activist orientation. i see this book as a complementary text that roughly acts as an introduction to theorizing aboriginal politics in canada and to positioning the contemporary moment. ideally, this provides a guide to action, a sense of what issues and battles are of greater urgency and perhaps some sense of how to intervene in an informed, reflective manner. like *the red indians*, i have kept this short so that it is accessible. and i have written it, as was the case earlier, without capital letters following the practice of bell hooks, of e.e. cummings, of all those who reject the symbols of hierarchy wherever they may be found.

i must apologize to métis readers: although i include a specific section on inuit, and much of the material bears on work with first nations across the mid and far north, i do not specifically offer any analysis that draws on the historical or contemporary positionality of métis. *the red indians* does include substantial material on métis history, but the accident of my own political engagements has meant i have not had the pleasure of working with some of the great métis leaders of our time. it is my preference not to report on trenches i haven't fought in.

i am a person of non-aboriginal descent who works professionally in the field of native studies and whose political activism is focused on indigenous issues. i have never apologized for this. if the very dire circumstances of the first peoples of canada are to ever meaningfully improve, we will need more people rather than less travelling down the road i and quite a few others have taken. i represent a recent iteration of non-aboriginal supporters of aboriginal leaders and communities in struggle, a lineage that stretches from even earlier than the late walter rudnicki and michael posluns and will stretch even further than to my young punk-anarchist colleagues in the winnipeg indigenous peoples solidarity movement. we need more rather than less joining us. we need a full-fledged movement; one that is mobile, flexible, ready to fight, and, critically, knowledgeable about the issues. i am certain aboriginal readers of these pieces will find something of value here, and hopeful that these words may play a small role in constructing a fragile but crucial alliance among canadians across the settler-colonial chasm.

finally, i wish here and now to express a few words of gratitude. i thank valerie zink for her encouragement and willingness to publish my work in *briarpatch,* from which chapter one of part one, "aboriginal rights are not human rights," developed. i'd also like to thank deb simmons— a longtime friend and colleague and comrade—who solicited my piece for *new socialist*, a revised version of which is chapter two of part one, "socialism and native americans." it was a friend and colleague, joyce green from the university of regina, who initially asked me to write what became the academic version, in *prairie forum,* of "aboriginal rights are not human rights," and i thank her for that and for her friendship. i take great pleasure in being able to express my longstanding appreciation to and admiration of cy gonick, who has enthusiastically supported the most wayward of my writings for *canadian dimension* and who has for decades embodied the gregarious, critical, persistent spirit of the left in our country. i am also very grateful to the manitoba research alliance for funding support that helped me prepare this manuscript; it is a great pleasure for me to be a part of an outstanding research team led by john loxley and including elizabeth comack, jim silver, ian hudson, shauna mackinnon, and lynne fernandez. les sabbiston helped with initial preparation of the manuscript. i thank peter ives for encouraging another arbeiter ring production on my part and for being a thoughtful interlocutor in my recent reading of the great italian marxist theorist antonio gramsci. josina robb is due profound thanks for a careful copy edit of the manuscript; and i must recommend the people at arbeiter ring to anyone who desires an audience of critical readers outside of academia; they are a pleasure to work with and have the highest professional standards. i also thank two scholars i respect and admire, james tully and glen coulthard, for valuable comments about the manuscript. my dear daughter, malay mary pilz (now a big girl!), knows that her every heartbeat fills my spirit with joy while my new son, joseph douglas, lifts it to heights beyond measure. all the love i have that remains i place tenderly at the feet of jaime drew.

part one: concerning aboriginal rights

the essays in this part make three interrelated points. first, the theoretical term "mode of production," used in marxist social theory, can ground a socialist theory and practice in relation to indigenous peoples' struggles in canada. second, aboriginal rights are therefore a critical legal tool in maintaining and revitalizing indigenous hunting modes of production in their resistance to capitalist and colonial totalizations. third, aboriginal rights must be sharply distinguished from human rights if they are going to be effective in such a role.

i. aboriginal rights and human rights: some thoughts

it's late august 2010 and i'm in the mackenzie mountains with my shuhtagotine (mountain dene) friends. after the craziest couple of hours on an all-terrain vehicle ride— crossing a small river that is almost deep enough to cover the tires of the little four-wheelers, and recrossing back and forth as we weave our way up the gravel, sand, and rock valley—we've parked the atvs at the foot of some hills near the source of the river and hiked up past the trees to the top of a ridge where we can find caribou. between berry and mushroom picking, fishing, and hunting moose and caribou, our growing camp at stewart lake is slowly getting well-stocked with food. on this day, sean etchinelle and i walk along high treeless ridges, not finding any caribou.

i've been thinking about why i'm here. a lot of my friends are jealous of my hunting stories, and though i've shot caribou and dall sheep without any qualms, i'm not a recreational hunter. i'm not here for the pleasure. i've been working with begade shuhtagotine (mountain dene of the keele river area) for more than 15 years now, often spending late summer immersed in the beauty of the mackenzie mountains: caribou flats far up the keele river, up the redstone river, at drum lake, at stewart lake. the begade shuhtagotine are dealing with an injustice: although the government claims they are signatories to the modern sahtu treaty, many of the begade refused as individuals to sign. that is, they have not signed up as beneficiaries of the treaties and have not received any of the benefits that they would be entitled to. they maintain, partly as a result, that they still have unsurrendered aboriginal title to their lands. it's a contemporary version of the lubicon cree story, and it shows that modern treaties are in many respects repeating the problems of earlier treaties. i've always felt that by going out on the land with hunters, i can learn about how these "big issues" and policies, such as the federal comprehensive land claims policy, affect people on the ground, on their ground, giving me insight into how all the abstract policy and theoretical issues actually work out in practice.

after hiking out of stewart lake, travelling by jet boat down the fast, shallow, gravel-bottomed keele river, then travelling by motor boat from tulita to pedzhi ke, where our vehicle is parked, i have time to think as the fourwheel drive negotiates the long straight stretches of the dusty gravel road. i'm trying to think of something to say about the united nations declaration on the rights of indigenous peoples (undrip), wondering if i have anything to say about it, when i have a eureka moment, an epiphany of sorts: someone—it could be me—should explain why aboriginal rights are not human rights.

i had always resisted working on aboriginal rights issues at the united nations level. i had seen some fairly talented people working, seemingly endlessly, through the 80s and 90s with little to show for their efforts. and, anyways, i had always had a fairly strong belief that aboriginal rights would be won or lost on the ground, at the grassroots level. so i've spent as much time as i can over the past three decades in small northern communities, providing free advice and helping build capacity

and networks among those who dissent with the existing policy framework. but then, after a deadline led to a
strong push, a declaration was finally passed by the united
nations general assembly in 2007. after that, i had joined
other canadian allies in insisting that canada adopt the
resolution, without actually reading the document closely
or thinking much about it. which, clearly, is a lesson: read
what you endorse before endorsing it!

when i did read it closely and think about it seriously,
i found that the undrip is a seriously flawed legal instrument. while it offers some very useful examples of specific
language around aboriginal rights issues, the undrip reflects a notion that all this time indigenous peoples around
the world were looking for human rights rather than aboriginal rights. the difference between these is not merely
academic. human rights, a product of the late 18th century
enlightenment, and of a long history of struggle, are rights
and freedoms that human beings enjoy inasmuch as they
are human. they tend to be used to protect individuals,
and tend to be invoked in urban contexts. everyone, on
principle, has access to them. they reflect a universalizing
notion of humanity, and involve equality rights and various freedoms that all humans should enjoy. this includes
indigenous peoples, inasmuch as they too, are human.

aboriginal rights, by contrast, are rights that only
certain people and peoples, indigenous peoples, have by

virtue of being indigenous. in effect, aboriginal rights reflect a notion of cultural particularism: indigenous cultures have become threatened as colonialism left many
indigenous peoples in the position of being a minority
in their homelands. we do not all have aboriginal rights.
nor should we. aboriginal rights stem from the struggles
of indigenous peoples. in a way they could be seen as a
specific form of customary rights, rights that developed
over time, through repeated practice of an activity, rather
than abstract rights that reflect a notion of how all people
are "the same." aboriginal rights have tended to be asserted
in rural contexts, and have tended to emphasize social collectives. by culture here i should stress that i am referring
to a broad beast: all those "ways" that mark the differences
between indigenous peoples and settler-newcomers. in
this book i use the term "mode of production" to analytically understand those differences, but here i will note that
culture in this materialist usage means ways of organizing
time, space, and subjectivity, it refers to forms of economic
activity (say, sharing) and forms of political activity (say,
participatory democracy). culture does not confine itself
to expressive activities—drum dances, language use, rega-
lia—but also involves economic activity and the practices
associated with indigenous sovereignty.

the reason this is not simply an academic issue is
that human rights can be used in justifying attacks on

aboriginal rights. in canada, that's what happened in 1968-69, when the federal government developed a set of policy proposals, called the white paper, which would have done away with all the aboriginal and eventually treaty rights of indigenous canadians. the proposals were intended to ensure that indigenous peoples in canada would become "equal" with all other canadians. a human right to equality became the battering ram that threatened to destroy any aboriginal rights. indigenous peoples in canada fought a bitter but eventually successful struggle, momentously defeating the white paper (at least as an official policy).

in the early 80s, when the canadian constitution was repatriated, aboriginal rights were included in a general way through section 35, which said simply but powerfully that "existing aboriginal and treaty rights are hereby recognized and affirmed." however, coming out of the white paper struggle, leaders knew that something else was needed to ensure such a proposal would never again be on the table. another section of canada's constitution, section 25, which has still received generally little academic or legal notice, was put in place in the charter of rights and freedoms. it says that the charter will not be interpreted in any way that might "abrogate or derogate," that is, diminish, aboriginal rights. by doing so, canada makes it clear that aboriginal rights have equal legal force with human rights, that human rights will not be used to override aboriginal rights.

the supreme court of canada has already drawn this distinction, writing in the 1996 van der peet decision that "aboriginal rights cannot, however, be defined on the basis of the philosophical precepts of the liberal enlightenment. although equal in importance and significance to the rights enshrined in the *charter*, aboriginal rights must be viewed differently from *charter* rights because they are rights held only by aboriginal members of canadian society. they arise from the fact that aboriginal people are aboriginal" (para 19).

there is no such language as can be found in section 25 of canada's constitution in the undrip. rather, the latter contains a long list of specified rights, some of them human rights and some of them aboriginal rights (both broad and particular), listed in a jumble, with no clause that protects aboriginal rights from the exercise of equality rights. in fact, most of the speeches that celebrated the passing of the declaration, and the undrip itself, tend to discuss it as an "extension" of the united nations universal declaration of human rights. extending universalism basically means assimilation: the precise approach that indigenous peoples have been fighting for hundreds of years. in van der peet, the supreme court also said that an aboriginal right protects a "practice, custom or tradition integral to the distinctive culture of the aboriginal group claiming the right." aboriginal rights protect what people have done, repeatedly, for many years; the activities or practices that reflect and/or express their culture. this includes how people make decisions and how they produce their livelihood as much as how they celebrate their spirituality or community.

it is easier to understand this from the mackenzie mountains than in the boardrooms of our cities. perhaps because when my shuhtagotine friends are out in their hunting camps they are both practising their aboriginal culture and exercising their aboriginal rights. it is easier to see this relationship out on the land, where it matters, than to discuss it in seminar rooms or read about it in the technical language of lawyers and scholars.

sean and i hear some shots. we rush down one ridge and, more slowly, up the next where we find sean's dad, david, has gotten two caribou. i make tea while sean and david butcher the caribou. a few days later i'll make the same trip with a larger group of younger people from our camp. it is my hope that there'll be shuhtagotine making this trip long after my time on this earth. they'll use different technologies, but will be hunting for the same animals in, if we leave the land intact, roughly the same places. it won't be the undrip, as currently written, that'll help them do so; and a lot of work needs to be done to identify and define aboriginal rights in the canadian constitution so as to give them more teeth. but at least the basic structure of our constitution reflects some hard-won understandings. including the idea that aboriginal rights are not human rights.

ii. socialism and native americans: a theoretical parenthesis

while socialists in canada have been strong supporters in solidarity struggles for social justice around the world, they have a less inspiring record when it comes to dealing with indigenous struggles in their own backyard. demonstrations against international colonialism, from the protests of recent imperial adventures in iraq and afghanistan to earlier mobilizations around south africa, el salvador, and east timor, seem to attract hundreds and sometimes thousands of dedicated activists. colonialism in canada's own far and mid north for many years, from the 70s through the late 90s, often drew a tepid response. the notable exceptions were mobilizations around hydro development in northern québec and the mackenzie valley pipeline proposals in the 70s. the crises at kanesatake in the early 90s did mobilize a significant youth-oriented activist support network, but it was really the arrest of the kitchenuhmaykoosib leadership in 2008 that led to the largest non-aboriginal solidarity protests around indigenous issues that canada had perhaps ever witnessed, providing something of a base for the groundswell of activism associated with idle no more in late 2012 that continues as i write. this is not to dismiss the efforts of earlier activists (among whom i include myself!) who supported the native trek in the early 70s, and organized around temagami, haida gwai, stoney point, grassy narrows, the lubicon, and so on. my forebears in the trenches at that time deserve a lot of credit for critical work that went largely unheralded in the mainstream. those earlier mobilizations, however, did not lead to anything like the mass outpouring of support that has emerged in the last 10 years.

the problem, in my view, signalled a failure of socialist, feminist, and other theory from the political left in canada to come to grips with the particularity of oppression here, a failure of the left to understand why they need to support and embrace an aboriginal and treaty rights agenda. this has been a particular pity because the left and aboriginal people in canada have a lot to say to each other, if they could really start talking. in what follows i would like to make a few points about history, class, social theory, and social activism in canada in the hopes of contributing to a stronger dialogue within the anti-capitalist movement about the critical place of aboriginal people to our struggle (and of our struggle to aboriginal people), and therefore the value of aboriginal rights in the context of a movement for socialism.

it is often and easily forgotten, a key part of the colonial sanctioned ignorance instilled through the dis-education system, that aboriginal peoples' labour ironically enough provided the fundamental productive value that established canada as an economically viable economy. aboriginal women and men were primary producers of fur for the first 300 years of colonization in canada. the forgetting of this fact of history has been a defining feature of many canadian nationalisms: capitalist, québecois, and many though not all socialist projects. this work did not constitute aboriginal people as a working class: whatever their position may have been they were clearly not wage workers forced to sell their labour power on an open market. they retained access to their own subsistence (the "means of production" in marx's terms) and retained through the whole period a strong sense of distinctiveness, grounded materially in a hunting economy. as the fur trade waned in centrality to the settler colony in the last half of the 19th century, aboriginal people were marginalized and processes of dispossession were deployed to immiserate them and to force them into the position of wage workers. marx recognized the centrality of such processes repeatedly in *capital*, arguing forcefully that the dissolution of the bonds between working people and their land was a central moment in the history of capitalism. he used the term "primitive accumulation" to describe this moment of capitalism, a moment that continues to the present day. i have called this moment "the racial reconfiguration and redistribution of wealth," because the land and community-based wealth of traditional indigenous peoples is reconstructed so it can become capital, and then appropriated by non-aboriginal people for their own benefit. such dissolutions of the ties to the land did not take place in a vacuum: they were hotly contested in the old world as in the new. in the new world, aboriginal leaders successfully deployed an array of tactics, ultimately codified in a doctrine of aboriginal rights, to maintain a degree of access to the means of subsistence. while relations between aboriginal people and newcomers for 300 years were primarily economic, organized around the dynamic of the fur industry, at the end of the nineteenth century a new logic began to prevail: relations came to be organized around politics. the canadian state became the key hegemonic institution in the lives of aboriginal people, as it remains to this day.

aboriginal people were therefore never a structurally significant part of the broad working class in canada. here and there, in this or that historical moment during the last 100-odd years, aboriginal people's labour-power was exploited and they fought back using the tools of working people. in large measure, particularly until indian act revisions in 1951 led to out-migration from reserves, aboriginal communities in the mid and far north stayed apart from the dramatic series of capital and labour confrontations that helped shaped critical aspects of canadian history. instead, they represented another track, one no less critical to capital development in canada and in my view no less critical to canadian history. aboriginal people maintained some degree of access and, in some cases, title to the land base that canadian and transnational capitalists salivated over. aboriginal and treaty rights were the legal means of protecting that access and title. in this resource-exporting nation the land base was central to the wealthy. clearing access to it has been one of the defining tasks of the canadian state. although increasing numbers of aboriginal people have joined the labour force in the past few decades, and although aspects of working class culture are embraced by aboriginal people (country music! hockey!), the defining struggles of aboriginal people have been over land use.

as i have argued elsewhere and will show below in a reading of the misguided book by frances widdowson and albert howard called *disrobing the aboriginal industry*, attempts on the part of the canadian left to neatly fit aboriginal people into the working class have not served to illuminate any dimension of aboriginal peoples' struggles and not given socialist practice a strong base from which to support those struggles. in many cases, the direct implication of this kind of class analysis is to imply that aboriginal peoples should give up their attempts to maintain

a subsistence economy, support whatever mining or pipeline or clear-cutting projects that are proposed for their
land, and join with other workers in carving out as good
a deal as is possible for themselves as workers. and this
means, materially, they should disadvantage themselves
in the struggle against capital by surrendering the ground
their ancestors fought to give them as a basis for maintaining a distinctive social identity, a distinctive way of life,
and a distinctive set of political and economic relations.

social theory does not have to fall into this trap. marx
himself offered a rich variety of concepts much more directly related to aboriginal peoples' struggles. these offer
socialists a strong position from which to articulate support for the particular struggles of aboriginal peoples. most
importantly, marx elaborated a notion of understanding
and classifying kinds of societies through the idea of the
mode of production as a defining feature. this allows us
to recognize that while a vibrant cultural diversity at the
level of expressive culture exists in aboriginal canada,
underlying the cultural diversity is a political-economic
similarity: aboriginal peoples belong to a hunting mode of
production. i refer to it globally as a "gathering and hunting mode of production" to foreground the importance of
women's labour as gatherers, though in the canadian north
we can use the term hunting cultures as a shorthand, since
gathering is less important to subsistence in that part of

the world. hunting peoples create and affirm social relations, political structures, and economic values that are antithetical to capitalism. these relations, structures, and values can be seen in the expressive culture: every fibre of a catholic ceremony instills notions of hierarchy and social passivity, while every fibre of a dene drum dance enunciates egalitarianism and participation, for example. as materialists, our concern is with the underlying political and economic relations, which, unusually for a marxist, i still insist on characterizing through the lens of cultural difference.

the word "traditional" is often invoked by the political right wing, say the bjp party in india or conservatives in canada and republicans in the u.s.a. today, to justify xenophobic and patriarchal practices and structures. but not all traditions are the same. some spring from the agriculture based-modes of production that predate capitalism and were often socially hierarchical and quite patriarchal. gatherers and hunters, whose cultures also predated capitalism, were, in contrast, egalitarian in social and gender terms. gatherers and hunters shared what they owned, and created a lifestyle that allowed for wealth in the form of time rather than in the form of things or money. hence social theory must reject the terms "precapitalist," "traditional," "premodern," or "tribal" as far too blunt a set of social instruments. the gap between agriculturalists and hunting peoples is a huge chasm that must be respected and understood. the struggle for aboriginal rights on the profoundest level is a struggle to carve a space and time for the continuance of hunting peoples' lifestyle and values in the world today. this point is made by hugh brody in his excellent book *the other side of eden*. such a cultural struggle is in its pores a struggle for sovereignty and the right to control economic resources: both are antithetical to the logic of capital accumulation.

conflicts between contemporary capitalism and aboriginal peoples need to be thought in terms of the developing and specific dominance of the former mode of production over the latter and in terms of the latter's resistance. marx also, especially in his understanding of the commodity and capital accumulation, understood how capitalism was a totalizing dynamic: it has to expand and absorb, ultimately erasing anything that acts as an obstacle to its rule. the "developing dominance" i referred to can also be called totalization: for aboriginal peoples a benign liberal democracy (as canada presents itself) is experienced as a totalitarian machinery devoted to the ruthless eradication of their life ways (a point i elaborate below). in his view of "primitive communism," guided by his reading of the anthropology of his time, marx articulated a notion that "early" forms of society could contain quite advanced social relations. it's actually interesting to scan his ethnographic notebooks and see references to "manitou" and various anishinabe and haudenosaunee teachings, something he devoted a good deal of time in his later years to understanding. it's also interesting to note that in his early years marx wrote about the customary rights of working people in much the same fashion that today we understand aboriginal rights. marx himself provides a much better place to begin an analysis of aboriginal politics in canada than many of the marxists who have followed in his wake.

where does this leave activists? if socialists do not want to repeat the mistakes of too many of their ossified ancestors they will have to engage in some rethinking. although they were not a working class in the nineteenth century, it is striking that in the production of belts made of buffalo hide that ran industrial machinery or whale oil that lubricated the same machinery, aboriginal peoples' labour and resources were near the core of the early accumulation of industrial capital. today the north american energy sector, in particular, which plays a key role in capitalist geopolitics and in the global economy in general, is looking northwards for oil, natural gas, and hydro electricity. aboriginal lands are again a critical stumbling ground in the drive to capital accumulation. and aboriginal life ways can be thought of not as sentimental holdovers of an outdated premodernism, but as the advance guard for the values we will all have to come to appreciate as human beings if we are to imagine a sustainable future; values, coincidentally, that line up far better with socialist ideals than many a more commonly referred to example of "real world" socialism.

so pay attention to the mighty deh cho and the mackenzie valley pipeline project. pay attention to the road that will push its way up the eastern side of lake winnipeg. pay attention to the hydro corridor that will bring ever more power to toronto, or minneapolis, or the eastern seaboard of the u.s. pay attention to the grand flooding that will take place in northern québec. and the diamond mines in the northwest territories and the nickel mines in labrador. and the clear-cutting in british columbia, in manitoba, in ontario. and uranium mining in baker lake. will this be the next few decades of canadian history? are aboriginal people involved in this history? are you sitting on the sidelines? you don't have to be. read some history. the treaties are a good place to start. read some anthropology. here and there, amidst all the kinship confusion, you can find some real inspiration. read some literature. there are some aboriginal novelists and poets who have more than a little to say about all this. aboriginal rights and treaty rights are the legal tools used by indigenous peoples in all these struggles. without understanding how people who belong to a different mode of production can resist capitalist colonial totalization through arming themselves with such a notion of rights, socialist supporters are tying their own hands behind their backs.

the notion of the nation, a continuing vexation for socialists, can be thought of in this light. the "first nations" clearly involve some kind of project to consolidate a national identity that enacts these life ways and values. such a project is always destabilizing for the broader project of nationalism in canada. just as the cree nation on the east side of hudson bay in their existence challenge a québecois national project, so the dene nation and the mohawk nation throw into question the canadian project. the canada that is a site for carefully orchestrated capital accumulation through "peace, order and good government" is antithetical to the democratic aspirations circulating in another country that exists within: i call it bush country. the canada that desires to be a site of democratic sovereignty in the face of imperial power will find inspiration and guidance in the practices of its despised margins.

one time i travelled to lac brochet, a dene community in the northwest corner of manitoba. they were then in receivership, officially seen by indian affairs as one of the most mismanaged communities in canada. in the week i was there, among many other meetings and gatherings, a community assembly was held. a strong proportion of the people came out. leaders were criticized, publicly.

decisions were made. this was a normal event in lac brochet, barely worth a passing comment to my friends who
live there. something called democracy, the vague ghost
of which barely survives in the marks some citizens make
every few years, was performed before my eyes, not for
my eyes but for itself. it is this, precisely this, that the
canadian state relentlessly works to stamp out. hence, the
first nations governance act of the late 90s: give them as
much bureaucracy as the rest of us suffer with. call that democracy. accountability. transparency. the new holy trinity
of capitalist politics, which capitalist politicians of course
feel no need to abide by, and capitalists themselves reject
as notions that have anything to do with how business is
run. hence also the recent bill 45 which makes it easier for
the working of capital on aboriginal lands. does the left
have anything to say about these colonial struggles?

socialists will appreciate that what is going on in
grassy narrows today is not some quaint environmental
struggle that they can add to their growing list of worthy
causes to be fit into the schedule where possible, another
addition to the long list in an ever extending rainbow co-
alition of "bigger tent" leftism. socialists are in a position
to understand which aboriginal projects, for all their new
age sensitivity, are engaged in a fundamental collusion
with capital and which, for all their inarticulate rage, are
engaged in a fundamental collision with capital. there are

more aboriginal people in cities than ever before. these people often cling fervently to their aboriginal identity, though their struggles are the struggles of poor people of colour and they can be identified as a segment of the working class. but numbers are not everything. the call of a very small part of the canadian population living in remote northern communities practising and embodying values that we can only dream of, that call for aboriginal rights must not be ignored by socialists or we will not deserve the name we give ourselves.

iii. aboriginal rights are not human rights

"politics is not made up of power relationships;
it is made up of relationships between worlds."
jacques rancière, *disagreement.*

as i've already noted, the growing discourse around aboriginal rights has suffered from a conceptual confusion between aboriginal rights and human rights. human rights have emerged from a european historical context and while they developed from the wrenching struggles of workers, women, and non-european peoples, they are inextricably linked to the notion of a universal humanity. while notions of universal human rights should not be lightly dismissed, they have on critical occasions served colonial projects by justifying interventions into indigenous practices. aboriginal rights were historically not an outgrowth of these struggles or even the western "march of progress," but rather emerged from indigenous community-based battles for land and culture. they must be conceptualized as cultural rights in the broad sense i have articulated above, that act to counterbalance universal notions of human rights with an appreciation for the cultural distinctiveness of indigenous peoples. in this chapter i will advance both a conceptual and historical argument pertaining to the difference and will then analytically specify human rights, aboriginal rights, and indigenous human rights. this chapter discusses in more detail the united nations declaration on the rights of indigenous peoples, the aboriginal rights provisions of the constitution of canada, a variety of legal decisions from canada and examples from indigenous communities and peoples in northern canada with whom i work.

the courts

in canada, the confusion can be traced (or became evident) in the late 60s through the decisions the supreme court was faced with in the drybones case and in the lavell/bedard cases. both of these cases dealt with the human rights of indigenous peoples.

the court was called on in 1969 to determine whether joseph drybones's conviction of an alcohol-related offence

under the indian act violated his human rights, since the
same offence would have resulted in a less severe punishment
to any non-aboriginal person under the laws of general application. while the case was a split decision, the debate was
over whether the then still relatively new bill of rights, a piece
of federal legislation, could be used to declare other pieces of
federal legislation, like elements of the indian act, inopera-
tive. there appeared to be little doubt that drybones had been
discriminated against and the majority ruled in his favour.

a few years later (1973), however, the court was faced
with virtually the same issue though in this event respecting
the question of discrimination against "indian" women who
lost their legal status as indians through marriage to non-
indian men. both jeanette lavell and yvonne bedard had
lost their legal status as "indians" because they married non-
indian men. both women took heart from the drybones
decision and tried to have it applied to their circumstances.
their cases were joined at the supreme court level. in another
narrow split decision the court reversed its position, deciding that the human rights bill could not overturn sections
of the indian act. but the 1973 decision was undoubtedly
also influenced by the national debate over aboriginal rights
occasioned by the struggle to force the federal government
to withdraw the 1969 white paper, and by the fact that the
court had some months earlier confronted the fact of the
existence of aboriginal title in the calder case.

the calder case (1973) was launched by the nisga'a first nation of bc, who asked the courts to recognize their un-surrendered aboriginal title to their traditional territory. although they lost the case on a technicality, the success of the nisga'a in having six out of seven judges say that aboriginal title grounded in prior occupancy continued to be a doctrine that had legal force in canada was a major step forward for aboriginal rights, but in some ways it also contributed to the confusion. legal commentators at the time, for example cumming and mickenberg, tended to argue that aboriginal rights derived from aboriginal title. arguably, aboriginal title could be seen as a way of securing (human) property rights of indigenous people. if everything, or in this case aboriginal rights, derived from aboriginal title then it would be possible to suggest that aboriginal rights in canada was, in a fairly esoteric but still discernable fashion, a form of human rights. the first major post-constitutional case, guerin (scc 1984)—involving a dispute in which a local indian agent had leased reserve land at a lower than market value—also lent support to this view, focusing on aboriginal title as a basis of the federal government's fiduciary responsibility.

the sparrow and sioui cases in 1990, on fishing and treaty rights respectively, did not touch on the issue because both were looking at aboriginal and treaty rights in the absence of discussion of title. it was possible, then, to start thinking along a different track. by 1994 i myself felt compelled, in my "theses on aboriginal rights" which introduced *unjust relations*, to argue that aboriginal rights were divided into two categories, property rights and political rights; that the latter did not derive from the former; and that "aboriginal cultures are the waters through which aboriginal rights swim" (12-13).

by 1996, in the van der peet trilogy of decisions (which included gladstone and smokehouse, all concerning the right to commercially harvest fish), the supreme court of canada had come to articulate the same view (needless to say without my having had any influence on the issue) and, more importantly, to clearly understand the difference between human rights and aboriginal rights. aboriginal rights were seen, like aboriginal title, to derive from the doctrine of prior occupancy. but title was not the basis of rights; rather, writing for a strong majority the then chief justice lamer stated "aboriginal title is the aspect of aboriginal rights related specifically to aboriginal claims to land; it is the way in which the common law recognizes aboriginal land rights" (para 33). furthermore, and famously in the case, aboriginal rights were effectively defined as follows: "in order to be an aboriginal right an activity must be an element of a practice, custom or tradition integral to the distinctive culture of the aboriginal group claiming the right" (para 46). this established that aboriginal rights were directly related to indigenous culture. since economic and political relations can be seen as "practices, customs or traditions," the court was at least implicitly endorsing the wide view of culture that i have deployed.

more importantly for our purposes here, in van der peet the justices, citing academic commentary, argued that "aboriginal rights cannot, however, be defined on the basis of the philosophical precepts of the liberal enlightenment. although equal in importance and significance to the rights enshrined in the *charter*, aboriginal rights must be viewed differently from *charter* rights because they are rights held only by aboriginal members of canadian society. they arise from the fact that aboriginal people are aboriginal" (para 19). by *charter*, of course, they mean the charter of rights and freedoms, which in canada is the constitutional instrument protecting human rights. inasmuch as this is clearly recognized by the judiciary in canada, it amounts to the argument of this book: aboriginal rights are not human rights.

theoretical histories: states and rights
viewed from one angle, the state itself, as a social construct, may be nothing more than an oscillation between the concentration of power and its limitation in the form of "rights." gathering and hunting peoples invented a form of sociality that did not depend on alien forms of condensed power (the state); communities involved intricate

webs of rights and responsibilities that were embedded in cultural practices such as ceremonies, naming, gift giving, food sharing, and socially extended responsibilities for child and elder care. tithe societies (see eric wolf 1982) involved state forms in which the sovereign did not enjoy absolute or totalitarian power (hence the development of "absolutism" was an aberration that needed to be named, which still included citizen rights, however uncodified). early western tithe society, the "ancients," codified and articulated property rights in the interest of social elites, but also developed mechanisms that defended popular rights (from elements of democracy in greece to the institution of republican government and later the tribunate in rome). throughout the history of ancient, medieval, and early modern tithe societies in the west, the state form tended towards a balance between something like near (but never wholly) absolute state power to structures that implicitly or explicitly limited state power (such as, famously, the *magna carta*). certainly the most absolute, or concentrated state power forms, tended to act in the interest of social elites and that meant the protection of private property. explicit private property rights were codified and were the subject of elite justification in philosophy.

it was popular struggle in combination with intellectual developments that led to the development of human rights. in the late eighteenth century, events in the united states of america, in france, and in haiti synthesized enlightenment ideals and popular political power, which came to be expressed in discursive notions of "rights," the rights of "man," as opposed to property rights. it is striking that slowly, the industrialization that developed in conjunction with this discourse gave the state greater tools to concentrate power, culminating in early forms of totalitarianism in the first half of the twentieth century. at the same time, the anti-slavery movement in the early nineteenth century, the women's rights (suffragette) movements in the later nineteenth and early twentieth century, and workers' movements through the nineteenth and twentieth century all deployed the language of rights as a tool to achieve their multi-variant popular objectives. emerging from these social movements, and in response to the horrors of fascist totalitarianism, the movement to codify human rights, as they became known, led to the famous 1948 united nations universal declaration of human rights. although these rights emerged from intense, popular struggles, in various places and phases of history they also offered a moral justification for elite-inspired colonial interventions, of the "white men saving brown women from brown men" sort that gayatri chakravorty spivak calls to our attention.

the universal declaration itself was a product of its high modernist era, reflecting an expanded notion of the "human" and a notion that state power had to be limited in a manner that expressed such "humanity." of course, this schematic theorization of the history of states and rights does appalling disservice to the texture of history, and does not represent anything like a fully enunciated theory of the state (or even the few-centuries-old capitalist state). but it has the merit of illustrating the popular base of human rights discourse and the continuing necessity of abstract, universalizing notions of human rights in the face of the newer technologies of state power and the newest state-sponsored juridical fictions that both deny basic human rights to some (labelled terrorists) while pretending to forcibly extend basic human rights (freedom and democracy) to others. it is also my hope that the narrative makes clear that the movement for human rights has not been a slow, liberalizing, progressive, inevitable triumphal procession. rather, if the rights-domination oscillation characterizes political society, in effect we are witnessing new institutions, new legal structures, new discourses, that replay ancient political contests.

i have fictioned a master narrative history of the world primarily to make this point: the united nations universal declaration of human rights has not and will not be the final stopping point on the path to social justice. nor will the canadian charter of rights and freedoms. with this backdrop, i turn to the specificity of aboriginal rights.

theoretical histories: customary and aboriginal rights

it is of more than passing interest that among karl marx's
earliest writings is a strong political and legal defence
of the customary rights of peasants to gather and use
deadwood, in which he deploys the phrase "from time
immemorial" (see 1975). marx was not entering a marginal
political sideshow in making these arguments (which he
himself later saw as a major turning point in his intellectual development) but rather joining in at the tail end
of a critical 18th and 19th century popular struggle for
what were called customary rights. in the english language, the historian of customary rights is e.p. thompson,
whose *customs in common* (1993) may ultimately eclipse
his other great study, *the making of the english working
class* (1963), and certainly should be read by any serious
students of indigenous rights. thompson emphasizes that
"the origin of common rights in royal or feudal grants
is a fiction" (133). rather, common rights derive from the
actual practices of people, whether in walking a particular
circuit to demonstrate their right of passage or to traverse
the passage itself, or in engaging in centuries-old subsistence activities: "perhaps in the first six decades of the
eighteenth century disputes about deer and other game,
about fishing rights, about timber, about the exploitation
of quarries, sand pits and peat, became more frequent and
more angry" (106).

what created these disputes was the totalizing spread of a quite different regime of property: "the concept of exclusive property in land, as a norm to which other practices must be adjusted, was now extending across the whole globe, like a coinage reducing all things to a common measure" (164). in the area of customary rights (and aboriginal rights), it is the state as an agent of totalization that matters. by the term "totalization" i refer to the whole painstaking historical process of reconfiguring notions and practices of space, time, and subjectivity in the modern period to accord with the new modalities for producing wealth: totalization: forms of practice, law, and the power to compel observance of these that spread across the globe over a period of a mere few centuries, and continue to spread both geographically and culturally. that spread is resisted, in the past and present, and the doctrines of customary and aboriginal rights are one of the baselines of such resistance. to a certain degree, the universal doctrine of human rights is complicit with this spread and in part explains some of the resistance to it. the british recognition of customary rights, through common law, is surely one of the grounds upon which, with the spread of british hegemony worldwide, the doctrine of aboriginal rights develops.

two small contrasting features of human rights and aboriginal rights may be worthy of notice here. on the one hand, human rights seem to develop, thrive, and be a site of struggle in the emerging and now dominant urban contexts associated with cosmopolitanism and liberal enlightenment. on the other hand, aboriginal rights, like customary rights, seem to be situated most often or tendentially in rural contexts, where ownership of the means of production for subsistence purposes remains viable. secondly, respect for human rights oscillates with a state power that at its extremity can be characterized as totalitarian (see arendt 1973), by which is meant a nearly all-pervasive exercise of state power. customary and aboriginal rights confront a state that instead serves the interest of totalization, by which is meant a state that works assiduously and relentlessly to establish cultural/material preconditions for capital accumulation. these two state forms have historically not frequently been co-existent, but when they are a whole new state of exception may emerge, threatening all forms of rights even as such state forms may deploy in orwellian manner the language of rights.

in this view, aboriginal rights are the customary rights of indigenous peoples. there is a performative element to aboriginal rights, inasmuch as they are grounded in the "embodied practices" (see taylor 2003) of indigenous peoples. this is one of the features foregrounded in the van der peet decision, discussed above.

historically, aboriginal rights in canada emerge from the struggle of indigenous peoples. the royal proclamation of 1763 itself was a response to pontiac's famous resistance a few years earlier (see hall 2003). while in the nineteenth century "indian rights," as they were then called, were clearly a part of the british north american, and later canadian, legal landscape, after the williams treaty in 1923 aboriginal rights were more often noted in the breach rather than through respect. this culminated in the "statement of the government of canada on indian policy, 1969" or now infamous "white paper," which in the name of equality (a human right) sought to remove all legal distinctions between "indians" and other canadians. in the intense struggle to prevent implementation of the white paper the term "citizens plus" (used in the early 60s by government officials and with a bit more prominence by h.b. hawthorn in his mid 60s report *a survey of the contemporary indians of canada*) was deployed to emphasize that indigenous peoples in canada were canadian citizens, had the human and citizenship rights of canadian citizens, but were also the bearers of something else, an unnamed "plus," that had to be acknowledged. the "plus" would come to be known as aboriginal rights. it was in this period of confusion and conflict that the drybones and lavell/bedard decisions were rendered; so too, the decision in calder, which marks a significant tipping point towards recognition of aboriginal rights, even if based primarily on title. the main point is that in canada, a deliberate attempt to—ruthlessly—extend human rights in the form of equality was placed in direct contradiction to the affirmative, differential rights doctrine embodied in aboriginal rights. it is ironic, years later, to see the united nations declaration on the rights of indigenous peoples characterized as an extension of the principle of human rights, an issue to be discussed below.

over the next decade legal and political attention in canada slowly turned to questions around aboriginal rights, prompted in part by their use by dene in the mackenzie valley pipeline conflict, by cree and inuit in the james bay and northern québec conflicts over hydroelectric production, and by the cree in northern manitoba dealing with similar issues (on the dene see watkins 1978, on cree in québec see richardson 1975, and on cree in manitoba see chodkeiwitz and brown 1999; in later chapters of this book i will discuss some of the recent struggles in northern manitoba to illustrate the points being made here). the original draft of the constitution that then prime minister trudeau wanted to repatriate contained no recognition of aboriginal rights. after another intense struggle including a first nations lobbying effort in westminster, section 35 recognizing and affirming aboriginal and treaty rights, which in the act follows after the charter of rights and freedoms, as well as section 25 which limits the exercise of the charter over aboriginal rights, were included. aboriginal rights were again a recognized, codified part of the political and legal landscape, though to what effect remains uncertain.

the confusion, again
even as careful, helpful, and astute an observer as the secretary general of amnesty international canada, alex neve, in a 2009 speech at the university of regina making a very strong argument in favour of the declaration, tends to confuse the issue of the relation between indigenous rights and human rights. his analysis is historically and politically compelling and valuable, while at the same time it is conceptually weak. i want to engage a close reading of his speech (published in a revised form in the same issue of *prairie forum* that the original version of this essay appeared) to demonstrate this issue, which is of critical importance. it should be noted, though, that amnesty international is a human rights-based organization with very little "track record" respecting aboriginal rights issues; if i am critical of neve it is as one of many, many examples i could draw upon of those that confuse human and aboriginal rights.

neve begins an extensive and very useful discussion of the 20-year history of the drafting of the declaration, itself prefaced by a discussion of the universal declaration of human rights and other human rights declarations, by mentioning in three places reasons why a declaration on the rights of indigenous peoples is needed. these are, in the first instance, "governments also recognized that some rights need extra attention, different attention or more detailed attention. that may be because of the heightened vulnerability of a particular group to serious human rights violations, such as women or children. or it may be because of the gravity or the insidious nature of a particular kind of human rights violations, such as racism or torture." this all deals with human rights violations, which may happen to indigenous people as well as others. secondly, again using the phrase "governments recognized," which leans towards the notion that rights emerge from liberal benevolence, neve states: "governments recognized that it was necessary to go further than the overarching human rights protections of the united nations charter, the universal declaration and the two covenants. they realized that the extent, longevity and entrenched nature of certain types of human rights violations is such that very specific and direct attention is inescapable." here, again, "human rights violations" is at issue, in this case the "extent, longevity and entrenched nature" of those being the specific issue. critically, neve situates the rights of indigenous peoples in subsidiary relation to "overarching" human rights. thirdly and finally, neve states:

and universally they are among the most marginalized and repressed members of the societies in which they live—subject to extreme levels of violence, violence that has possibly reached the level of genocide in some countries over the decades and centuries; living in extreme poverty; coping with relentless encroachment upon and theft of their traditional lands; and facing a range of sometimes brutal, often insidious laws, policies and practices aimed at suppressing and eradicating indigenous culture, language and way of life.

again, most of this specifically details human rights abuses; at the very end he tacks on the notion of "often insidious laws, policies and practices aimed at suppressing and eradicating indigenous culture, language and way of life." culture, the basis of what makes indigenous peoples distinct and the basis of aboriginal rights, belatedly makes it into the picture.

this conceptual confusion, and emphasis on the human rights of indigenous people with a minimal appreciation for the notion of cultural distinctiveness as an underlying element of aboriginal rights, leads neve down a path that ultimately vitiates much of his concern for indigenous peoples as indigenous peoples. hence, for example, "that there was early recognition that the rights of indigenous peoples merited special attention *within* the united nations human rights system: that the nature, scale and severity of the violations were such that it was not enough to rely only on the universal guarantees of equality and justice contained in the charter, declaration and the two covenants" (emphasis added). without a notion of the particularity of aboriginal rights, neve never notices that universal human rights may often provide the explicit justification for trumping aboriginal rights, as nearly happened in the struggle over the white paper in canada. by situating aboriginal rights "within" the united nations human rights system, the united nations effectively ensures that aboriginal rights take second place: that universality will always hold the deciding cards over cultural difference, including cultural difference in political and economic spheres of activity. this is a problem with the declaration itself, and one that neve never addresses, but a problem to which we will shortly turn our attention. neve is clearly not the only one to turn a blind eye to the issue: neve notes approvingly that "australia's minister of indigenous affairs, jenny macklin, called the declaration a 'landmark document that reflects and pays homage to the unique place of indigenous people and their entitlement to all human rights as recognized in international law.'" the entitlement of indigenous people to "all human rights" is not the same as the question of aboriginal rights.

interestingly, neve refers in three places in his article to the "aspirational" nature of the declaration, for example emphasizing at one point "the aspiration[al], non-binding nature of the declaration." in fact, the declaration on the rights of indigenous people never uses the term "aspirational." it does "proclaim" the declaration as a "standard of achievement to be pursued in a spirit of partnership and mutual respect" (16). whether a "standard of achievement to be pursued" is the same as an "aspirational, non-binding" statement is open to interpretation. he notes that in most instances declarations get turned into more binding documents called covenants. however, it is striking that months after his speech, when canada finally responded to the pressure he and many others brought to bear on it for not adopting the declaration, it did so as an "aspirational" document rather than as a "standard of achievement to be pursued." neve, in effect, let the canadian government off the hook even before it was hooked!

the united nations declaration on the rights of indigenous peoples

it is striking that the document is itself called the united nations declaration on the rights of indigenous peoples. syntactically, this leaves open the question of whether it is affirming indigenous (aboriginal) rights, or the human rights of indigenous peoples. "the rights of indigenous peoples" as a phrase may be used to characterize either or both of these forms of rights. in this instance, as articulated through the declaration itself, it means both.

the united nations declaration on the rights of indigenous peoples, as it is introduced in the english-language text, states that indigenous people are "among the most impoverished, marginalized and frequently victimized people in the world. this universal human rights instrument is celebrated globally as a symbol of triumph and hope." throughout the introductory material and the document itself, it is positioned as an extension of the doctrine of universal human rights, rather than a document of equal or counterbalancing weight. for example, the statement of victoria tauli-corpuz, the chair of the united nations permanent forum on indigenous issues, on the occasion of the adoption of the declaration, declares that the moment "marks a historical milestone in its long history of developing and establishing international human rights standards." this confusion is also reflected in many of the "supportive statements" appended to the declaration.

perhaps another way i can make the issue clear is with reference to the aboriginal rights legal structure, let's call it a topography, embedded in the constitution of canada. there, it is recognized that the human rights embedded in the charter of rights and freedoms could be interpreted in a manner that would diminish aboriginal rights. section 25 of the charter therefore states that "the guarantee of this charter of certain rights and freedoms shall not be construed so as to abrogate or derogate from any aboriginal, treaty or other rights or freedoms that pertain to the aboriginal peoples of canada." philosophically, this is a substantial step ahead of the declaration, because it reflects the notion that universalist equality rights can be deployed in a way that would diminish the force of aboriginal rights. in fact, in the corbiere case (1999), involving whether off-reserve indians could run for office and vote in on-reserve elections, which has been the only supreme court of canada case to pay significant attention to section 25, a significant minority of the court suggest that the canons of interpretation of section 25 are such as to give it even more scope for application than the actual aboriginal rights recognition clause that is more frequently invoked, section 35. there is no such legal topography at work in the united nations declaration. the universal declaration includes no clauses limiting its application over culturally distinct indigenous peoples.

instead, the united nations insists that the rights of indigenous peoples are an extension of universal human rights, and is explicit that the newly gained rights must be brought within the scope of the older doctrine. the three sections of article 46 in the declaration make this clear. section 1 establishes that "nothing in this declaration may be interpreted as implying for any state, people, group or person any right to engage in any activity or to perform any act contrary to the charter of the united nations" (39);

section 2 of that article states that "in the exercise of the rights enunciated in the present declaration, human rights and fundamental freedoms of all shall be respected" (39); and section 3 makes it clear that "the provisions set forth in this declaration shall be interpreted in accordance with the principles of justice, democracy, respect for human rights, equality, non-discrimination, good governance and good faith" (40). the notion that the rights of indigenous peoples, inasmuch as they are aboriginal rights, might be seen as forms of positive discrimination, is therefore entirely absent from the overall topography of the declaration. also absent is the notion that human rights, especially equality rights, may sometimes be deployed to limit or render meaningless aboriginal rights, or any notion that aboriginal rights might be viewed specifically as a counterforce to human rights.

this is not to say that the declaration is not a worthy achievement; nor to imply that it should not be adopted and implemented; nor to assume it will not be of any value in the struggle of indigenous peoples. indigenous peoples do need to have their human rights respected. getting acknowledged or recognized at the united nations level does represent an achievement of lasting value. but, as indigenous peoples, for their aboriginal rights to have any legal strength in the struggle to help them retain their distinctive cultures, they need a version of aboriginal rights that cannot be "trumped" by universalisms. the declaration is a flawed tool for respecting and affirming global aboriginal rights.

reading the united nations declaration on the rights of indigenous peoples

in my reading of the document, the human rights of indigenous peoples are the clear subject of ten articles (1, 2, 6, 17, 21, 22, 23, 43, 44, and 46). articles that in some way or other deal with culture, tradition, language, or indigenous institutions and laws, and may therefore be interpreted as relating to aboriginal rights as i have characterized them following the logic of canadian jurisprudence, are the sole subject of twenty articles (3, 4, 5, 8, 9, 11, 12, 13, 14, 16, 19, 20, 24, 25, 31, 33, 35, 36, 37, and 40). an additional nine articles pertain to both human rights of indigenous peoples and aboriginal rights (7, 15, 18, 34, 38, 39, 41, 42, and 45). finally, a full seven articles deal with land rights and aboriginal title, which again could be seen as belonging to either form of right, or even to property rights (10, 26, 27, 28, 29, 30, and 32). note the way in which these issues are mixed; the authors of the declaration had no sense of the ways in which some of the first set of rights might be deployed to limit the second set. there is no coherent notion that these forms of rights should be grouped as sets.

i'll give an example to make this clear. article 21, which i have situated in the category of human rights, deals broadly with the economic well-being of indigenous peoples. it makes provision that:

> 1. indigenous peoples have the right, without discrimination, to the improvement of their economic and social conditions, including, inter alia, in the areas of education, employment, vocational training and retraining, housing, sanitation, health and social security.

> 2. states shall take effective measures and, where appropriate, special measures to ensure continuing improvement of their economic and social conditions. particular attention shall be paid to the rights and special needs of indigenous elders, women, youth, children and persons with disabilities.

the eurocentric nature of the language being deployed here demands some attention: the united nations document does not invoke any greeting or thanksgiving in any indigenous language. it does use "inter alia" (among other things), thus giving additional attention to latin, a dead but hardly uninfluential language (i note that i myself on rare but significant occasions have been known to resort to latin numerals). it does not develop or rely on a single concept from within a single indigenous worldview. since it cannot decide which one to use, it uses none; this particular bit of eurocentrism is a travesty.

of special concern is the way this list in article 21 (vocational training!) and the standards it implies could patently justify, in the name of the rights of indigenous peoples, state interventions: building a hydroelectric dam can be justified for the jobs it creates; removing children can be justified to improve their educational attainment or social circumstances within the mainstream of society. while there are other clauses that mitigate against these effects, by placing the document as a whole within and underneath the logic of overarching, universal human rights, where there is a conflict it appears clear that indigenous human rights will over ride aboriginal rights, to the likely detriment of indigenous people. this latter is likely since it is "states" that will tend to implement the human rights.

state involvement is not a question of no importance here. the declaration contains a number of clauses that deal with self-determination, including four in a row at one point. these are:

> *article 3* indigenous peoples have the right to self-determination. by virtue of that right they freely determine their political status and freely pursue their economic, social and cultural development.

> *article 4* indigenous peoples, in exercising their right to self-determination, have the right to autonomy or self-government in matters relating to their internal and local affairs, as well as ways and means for financing their autonomous functions.

article 5 indigenous peoples have the right to maintain and strengthen their distinct political, legal, economic, social and cultural institutions, while retaining their right to participate fully, if they so choose, in the political, economic, social and cultural life of the state.

article 6 every indigenous individual has the right to a nationality.

what is important is what is missing from this list. indigenous people do not have a right to sovereignty. further, they only have the "right to autonomy or self-government in matters relating to their internal and local affairs." interestingly, articles 11 to 17 begin with a first clause, "indigenous people have the right," and add a second clause, "states shall" (articles 21, 22, 26, 29, 30, 32, and 36 use the same formal structure; articles 18 and 19 use the form in separate articles). the declaration posits a bifurcated world, with indigenous people on one side as rights holders and the state on the other as duty bound. it is clear that forms of self-government are to exist within the existing state system. although the declaration places clear demands on states vis-à-vis their practices respecting indigenous peoples, it also enforces the notion that indigenous people are ultimately under the aegis or authority of existing national states, and there they must stay. even aspirationally.

this is, again, not to say that the declaration is in broad historical terms of no positive political and legal value, even in the canadian context. there are 20 clauses that specify aboriginal rights, and these are not a part of the canadian, or many other, legal/political contexts. for example, as well as article 44 guaranteeing that the rights of indigenous peoples are available equally to indigenous male and female persons, a clause in article 22 mandates that "states shall take measures, in conjunction with indigenous peoples, to ensure that indigenous women and children enjoy the full protection and guarantees against all forms of violence and discrimination." another article, 33, specifies rights to control citizenship among indigenous peoples as follows:

> 1. indigenous peoples have the right to determine their own identity or membership in accordance with their customs and traditions. this does not impair the right of indigenous individuals to obtain citizenship of the states in which they live.

> 2. indigenous peoples have the right to determine the structures and to select the membership of their institutions in accordance with their own procedures.

both of these, and many others of the 20 articles that deal with aboriginal rights, could be important tools in litigations or in social justice struggles in canada; where the state, through the indian act, still ultimately controls the legal status of first nations citizens, and where gendered violence against aboriginal women remains a pathological and deeply repulsive feature of the dominant society. i should also acknowledge that the declaration is the culmination of a very long struggle, and is justly celebrated by indigenous activists as a moment in which the existence of aboriginal peoples is recognized and validated by the global community.

a conceptual structure

with this as background, it should be clear that some conceptual clarity is demanded on issues pertaining to aboriginal rights, particularly in order to understand how they can come into conflict with human rights. human rights, citizenship rights, and property rights operate and intersect on one plateau of rights discourse. aboriginal rights, customary rights, and treaty rights operate on another. indigenous human rights, as an application, can be specified with reference to both, though in my view they belong with the first set.

on one plateau, then, are the set of rights that may be enjoyed by individuals by virtue of their citizenship, their humanity, and their wealth. citizenship rights are the national rights enjoyed by people and individuals through being entitled members of a nation. these may include rights to participate in that nation's political system and rights to be protected, internationally, by representatives of their nation. these rights vary dramatically, as different nations clearly have different abilities to protect their citizens and have different status in the global hierarchy of national polities. these were the forms of rights that edmund burke famously preferred to "the rights of man" being proclaimed by the revolutionaries in 18th century france. human rights are rights and freedoms that belong to all peoples inasmuch as they are human. human rights involve equality rights, individual freedoms, and rights to belong to cultural and national collectivities. national collectivities may, and often do, enshrine human rights as an aspect of the rights of their citizens, as the canadian charter of rights and freedoms example suggests. property rights speak to the security of property ownership, and may be a form of human rights and/or a form of citizenship rights. the doctrine of property rights has tended to protect the wealthy of the world as individuals, but it can pertain to collectives in the forms of intellectual property, cultural property, and aboriginal title. property rights, in the capitalist world, in effect establish the preconditions within which citizenship and human rights operate.

aboriginal rights are rights that pertain to a specific group of people, frequently the prior occupants of a territory in pre-colonial times, and are therefore established on a wholly distinct plateau of rights: they do not belong to everyone. aboriginal rights exist in order to acknowledge the cultural distinctiveness of prior occupants. thus they tend to be collective, and particular. they may be seen as a variety of customary rights, tied as they are to the collective cultural traditions and practices of specific indigenous peoples. any peoples who have engaged in a practice for such a lengthy period that they have earned a right to continue the practice may enjoy customary rights. treaty rights are any rights that may be conferred through negotiations between a specific indigenous people and a specific nation-state. in this perspective, aboriginal rights might be seen as the legal toolkit that protects the specific cultures, associated with specific modes of production, of indigenous peoples.

the human rights of indigenous peoples involve the application of human rights to indigenous individuals. they belong on the territory of human rights, but involve the people associated with aboriginal rights. obviously, indigenous peoples can have their rights as human beings violated. although in effect the universal declaration of human rights should be sufficient to protect indigenous peoples, the reasons alex neve sets out for the declaration amount largely to a justification of elaborating and extending human rights specifically to indigenous peoples. but it must be clear by now that this is a different ethical, legal, and political issue than the issue of aboriginal rights.

aboriginal rights exist for the protection of the cultural distinctiveness of indigenous peoples, in the recognition that such distinctiveness may be of value in a rapidly changing world. they therefore pull in a different direction than human rights. human rights move towards what is common in humanity and are an expression of some basic ideas thought to be of universal value. aboriginal rights move in the direction of what characterizes specific groups of people and of what defines them as distinct, especially at the glacial, or epochal, level of modes of production. the actual practices protected by aboriginal rights are particular and vary from group to group, perhaps from time to time. human rights work to abstract from particular actions and protect a broader principle embedded in the action (for example, freedom of speech).

the problem that emerges is that human rights may be used to override aboriginal rights. human rights can easily become a weapon of totalizing states in their war against land-based, self-sufficient, indigenous communities. a young man is taken from his home to an island, where he is left isolated for several days as a first stage of initiation into a dance society. his human rights were clearly violated, in the interests of the aboriginal rights of his nation. as it happens, respect for individual autonomy is an element of the cultures associated with a gathering and hunting mode of production, to a far greater extent than the notions enshrined in human rights discourses. but that does not mitigate the fact that the two, aboriginal and human rights, do not sit comfortably side by side. the united nations structure establishes a hierarchy, with human rights on the ascendance. the rights of indigenous peoples are positioned as an extension of human rights. they are not.

the particular cultures of gathering and hunting peoples, one specific form of indigenous peoples (who are at some times and in some places agriculturalists and in other times and other places gatherers and hunters), often as i've noted, show great respect for the "autonomy of the individual." in fact, since property rights are less paramount, oftentimes gatherers and hunters enacted cultural mechanisms that showed greater respect for equality and freedom than the most "advanced" liberal democracies of our own time. yet, still bound by the notion that "we," the advanced, progressive, developed west, know more than "they," "we" insist on imposing our hierarchies in the name of equality and freedom. to repeat: we insist on imposing our hierarchies in the name of equality and freedom; this, in part, is what the united nations declaration on the rights of indigenous peoples amounts to; our notion of human becomes the notion of human, our notion of freedom and equality becomes the notion of freedom and equality, our notion of rights is the only notion possible.

from the ground up

just as human rights exist more in the breach than in the enforcement, many years after the universal declaration of human rights was promulgated and even after the covenants meant to give it force were passed, so too aboriginal rights continue to be violated on a daily basis. they are violated here in canada, part of the "advanced," "developed," "progressive" social world as much as they are in many other parts of the world. when the united states, at the pinnacle of the world hierarchy, feels free to entirely violate basic human rights in the interest of its war on terror, it is difficult to feel optimistic about global compliance with human rights instruments. it is even more difficult to be optimistic about the aboriginal rights provisions in a document as compromised as the united nations declaration on the rights of indigenous peoples.

in august, 2010, i was in the mackenzie mountains with shuhtagotine, mountain dene from the village of tulita. my students and i discussed and argued about the status and role of dene women in the hunting camp. we negotiated our own role and status among the generations of hunters present with us. we went on crazy rides on all terrain vehicles, across rivers and up riverbeds into the foothills and past the trees high onto mountains in search of caribou. we traded stories and borrowed rifles and lent fishing rods and helped each other in the daily routines of a work that is somehow more like leisure and a leisure that is somehow more like work than we imagined. we drank water taken straight from the lake and ate fish from the nets or caribou from our hunts. we kept watch for moose and went on dusk and dawn excursions to see if we could find them out in the open. we learned a little bit about what it is to be dene. and, by doing so, perhaps we learned a little bit more about what it is to be human.

aboriginal rights get asserted this way, in the practice of indigenous culture. they will, in the end, not be handed down from on high as a gift from the king or the united nations (one of e.p. thompson's points about customary rights). they are won in blockades, in occupations, in marches and walks, through patience and practices, through petitions, through the determination and strength of indigenous nations and their allies. critically, aboriginal rights are achieved through the enactment of cultural practices, through the repetition of political and economic and social and spiritual and expressive activities that were engaged in, albeit with different technologies, ecological, and social contexts, many, many years ago. these practices, paradoxically, may also have something to teach about such cherished human rights as equality and freedom. but when we arrogantly impose our universality, we blind ourselves to the possibility of learning, even learning what it is to be human.

the declaration presumes indigenous peoples as victims and as weak. in the various rationales and justifications, it always positions indigenous peoples as in need of benevolent support. nowhere does it recognize the strong contribution that indigenous peoples as indigenous peoples make to the world. it comes closest to doing so in its preamble, but adopts instead the phrase: "all peoples contribute to the diversity and richness of civilizations and cultures, which constitute the common heritage of humankind." in other words, all peoples, including indigenous peoples, have a contribution to make: there is nothing especially valuable about indigenous knowledges and cultures. the preamble deploys this, too, as a critical fiction. that "we" in the "advanced," "developed," "progressive" world might actually have something to learn from indigenous peoples, might have something to gain by living side by side in peace with thriving indigenous cultures, appears unthinkable among the too many, too smart jurists of universalism. nowhere does the united nations appear to imagine *pimatisiwin*, the good life, which may be found in andean and mackenzie mountain ranges. until they can, their declarations will float lightly on currents of rising air, never finding the ground beneath their feet.

iv. the emperor's old clothes

to show how misguided a purportedly socialist analysis is
when it imposes a narrow class analysis on indigenous communities and ignores the concept of mode of production, and
how such an approach can have no appreciation for concepts
of aboriginal or treaty rights, we can engage in the admittedly
painful process of reading *disrobing the aboriginal industry:
the deception behind indigenous cultural preservation* by frances
widdowson and albert howard (mcgill-queen's, 2008). this
book purports to be a kind of "exposé" of the use of aboriginal
traditional knowledge in policy making and ranges far afield
into a critique of the idea of indigenous rights and a survey of
problems in the fields of aboriginal healthcare, education, self-
government, land claims, and so on. i had previously written
these authors off as "kooks" from the far political right wing;
but now they have been embraced by certain prominent left
academics, and have themselves started to gloss their opinions
with marxist rhetoric. their work does an enormous disservice
to the growing movement of socialist activists and theorists in
canada who are engaged in the real work of decolonization,
and could potentially set back a growing oppositional movement for years. if widdowson and howard's book has any
value for the left, it is as a clear marker of the path not to take.

the authors tout their experience working with the
government of the northwest territories as a basis that inspired the study, beginning with an anecdote from their

time there. i, myself, would not be so proud of working as a bureaucrat for a colonial institution. the two have no actual community-based experience that they refer to, and may very well have never spent a night in an aboriginal community. their analysis, to the extent they have one, is that indigenous peoples' human rights are being violated; as communities they suffer from a "developmental gap" that needs to be closed; and that presumably they should join a struggle with other working-class peoples for better wages and conditions of work.

thus the agenda of the book is to attack the notion of aboriginal rights in favour of a notion of universal human rights. the book dismisses aboriginal culture as "primitive" and outdated, and relies on the evolutionary anthropology of a century ago. its particular target is traditional knowledge—especially traditional ecological knowledge, which they argue does not exist except as forms of local knowledge that people from any culture can have. their argument illustrates the degree to which an understanding of the difference between aboriginal rights and human rights is not merely academic hairsplitting but has significant real-world consequences. a human rights agenda must inevitably dismiss aboriginal cultural distinctiveness and align, as widdowson and howard do, with a totalizing state, itself eager to "close the developmental gap" in the interest of full cultural assimilation.

this book is also based on intellectual dishonesty. the authors can barely cite a living anthropologist who will agree with them, so the anthropologists they cite favourably almost all come from before the 1950s, when the now totally discredited doctrine of social evolution still left traces of its pernicious influence. they make arguments that have been entirely discredited and understood as racist for 50 years. the dishonesty comes through, because in each chapter where they tackle an issue, they refuse to actually grapple with the stronger scholars who deal with the subject matter, usually relying on newspaper accounts and non-academic works to act as straw dogs they can knock over. for example, the chapter on "justice" (they mean criminal justice; the idea of justice is foreign to this book) offers one dismissive paragraph to rupert ross's carefully conceived arguments about traditional justice based on his lifetime of work as a crown prosecutor. the chapter on environmental management dismisses harvey feit and fikret berkes in a single paragraph, never coming to serious grips with the elaborate and compelling arguments of those scholars, and instead implies with no evidence that their work is based on a kind of "new age" spirituality (it is not). rarely do they actually confront strong versions of the arguments they oppose. although they frequently gloss from james a. clifton's book, *the invented indian* (much of their own work is a coles notes version of it), to "debunk" what they perceive as myths about indigenous contributions to contemporary life, they are quite happy to regurgitate myths like that of the bloody falls massacre, which 20 years ago scholars realized was largely an invention of samuel hearne's london editors (they cite hearne uncritically).

they are worried about being called racists, so they try to inoculate themselves from the charge by confronting it. they argue that they never presume an inherent racial difference; rather, all people are equal, and it is only the "developmental gap," the nostalgic attachment of aboriginal leaders and supporters of a romantic vision of aboriginal culture, that is responsible for the "social dysfunctions" they see in all those communities they never bothered to visit. again, seeing cultural difference as a valid expression of differing modes of production is anathema to their own romantic attachment to contemporary capitalist culture. it is true that much of their argument, technically, is ethno-centric rather than racist: it presupposes the superior value of capitalism (a strange idea for alleged marxists to have) to "earlier" forms of social organization (unlike marx, who always noted—even within the evolutionary anthropology he accepted—that "earlier" forms of society were far advanced when it came, for example, to community relations). and of course, the notion of different modes of production that deploy radically different social logics is beyond their very limited horizons of thought.

there are moments, however, when their ethnocentrism does slide over into overt racism, like when they begin chapter 10, on traditional knowledge, with a discussion of the book *why cats paint*, effectively implying that elders have the same absence of ability to think as cats have to create art (offering shades of sepúlveda's comparison of indigenous peoples to monkeys back in the mid 16th century, which is about where this book belongs).

there is a more pernicious racism when they name many aboriginal leaders and gleefully "out" them for problems of alcoholism and sexual abuse. the book contains one mention of residential schools, and never draws any connections. by implication, they charge that the vast majority of aboriginal leaders are corrupt and morally bankrupt. these parts of the book read so distastefully that it is difficult not to feel "slimed" simply in allowing one's eyes to slide over these pages. they never mention conrad black or brian mulroney, those standard-bearers of the high moral values of contemporary culture. and they smugly, simply, and blithely assume their own middle-class moral superiority.

here and there, as in the closing two paragraphs of the introduction and the last paragraph of the book, they refer to themselves as historical materialists, and they refer to marx. these read like graft-ons, and are generally out of tune with the rest of the text. but these authors are not in any way dissidents. if all of marxism gets tarred by this brush, we will have set back the critical cause of forging an indigenous alliance with labour, a cause that offers real potential to destabilize the current capitalist regime in canada.

actually, the book is guilty of a worse crime than its widespread ethnocentrism and more occasional racism: stupidity. for example, the "disrobing" in the title is a reference to the story of the emperor's new clothes. they feel compelled to actually tell that story, duly citing hans christian andersen, which is about the level of their overall "analysis." i found myself keeping a list of howlers as the only entertainment i could give myself as i read this. among the many, many examples i could cite is this precious bit of text: they write, in an insipid and long outdated discussion, of the way certain changes led to "a significant advancement [advance is not enough!] in technology and facilitated the transition to food production" (12). "the transition to food production!" i fear life before food production must have been truly miserable...

their "what is to be done" concluding chapter says nothing, except that the task is to reduce the "developmental gap" that holds aboriginal people back. uh, actually guys, this is what the federal government has been trying to do since about, um, 1867! so it's not really a new idea, nor one that has proven effective; it has been responsible for producing much of the misery that exists today. but they blithely ignore what is historically inconvenient to their argument—namely, history. historical materialism begins, actually, with the concept of mode of production.

very few on the left will take anything but offence from their words, but many on the right will happily wield them as weapons against the long-unfolding struggle for aboriginal rights. at the current historical moment, we are at a critical crossroads in that struggle. in australia, aboriginal people literally faced away from then prime minister howard, turned their back on him, when he spoke to them in the waning years of his reign. i suggest we socialists who actually work with actual communities turn our back on this text and these writings. let them be embraced and nurtured by the political reactionaries they belong with and these books, like flanagan's *first nations? second thoughts,* sink out of sight. in its sloppiness, ethnocentrism, racism, and stupidity, this book does not reflect well upon its authors, the readers who endorsed it, the editors who proofread it, the scholars who supported it, and the publisher who will allow this book to stand on their shelves next to the many excellent books in their native and northern series.

part two: 50 years of struggle

in this part, i turn to the nexus between recent history, politics, and law. it is important for socialists to not theorize from the air, but look at what aboriginal political leaders who deserve our respect have actually been doing: their successes and failures, their goals and obstacles. one of the pitfalls that widdowson and howard's book demonstrates is how dangerous and counterproductive a high-sounding principle, say "equality" to choose one i personally admire, can become when brandished from the clouds of a theory that never touches the ground. part two begins with a chapter covering the period from 1963 to 2003 and shows the way grassroots struggles interact with legal challenges in each of the decades in question. the next chapter, "inuit country," describes the specific cultural, historical, legal, and political situation of canada's inuit people. inuit are so far removed from the mainstream that we sometimes forget that they too are on a front line of anti-capitalist resistance. i follow this with another historical overview, this time regarding aboriginal title, one of the most important aboriginal rights and certainly one which merits some specific attention. the chapter called "the violence of the letter" focuses on treaties and land claims. i then turn briefly to show what a policy framework that respects aboriginal rights would look like in a chapter called "towards a new policy paradigm for first peoples." finally, to somewhat update the narrative of political struggle, the last chapter, "turning the page on colonial oppression," looks at two more recent political developments: the vancouver meeting of a nascent national network called the defenders of the land and the emergence of the idle no more movement.

i. 50 years in indian country

the past 50 years have seen dramatic changes among the aboriginal peoples of canada. in 1963 the legacy of colonialism was deeply entrenched, aboriginal peoples were seen as a "problem population" within canada, aboriginal rights were widely ignored and unknown, there were few national voices or forums for aboriginal leaders. as i write this, the struggle to decolonize is being engaged in a wide variety of institutions. aboriginal people have made outstanding and widely appreciated contributions to canadian art and culture; aboriginal rights are enshrined in the constitution; well established major national and regional aboriginal political organizations provide strong and vocal leadership. while this is not a history of how "every day and in every way things have gotten better and better," the gains that have been made should be celebrated as much as we might observe how more deeply insidious colonial processes have become.

three broad themes can be pointed to at the outset. the first is that for the most part the struggles of aboriginal peoples have directly focused on the state rather than capital. although the state has acted as an agent of capital, working assiduously on many fronts and levels to "total-ize" aboriginal peoples, and although capital itself has been directly involved in some of the resource conflicts that gained prominence, it remains notable that the struggle has been almost exclusively with policies and agents of the state. secondly, there has been a cycle of escalating violence over the four decades that will be of concern to any who watch this particular politics. from the confrontation on parliament hill in 1974, through to the murder of dudley george at stoney point in the 90s, the state's willingness to use violence has partly fed renewed aboriginal militancy with increasingly troubling results. thirdly, the complex-ity of this domain can hardly be overstated: aboriginal peoples' struggles have involved significant tensions over gender equality issues, an intricate relation between institutions and local communities, serious disjunctures and engagements between the overlapping domains of law and politics, and growing diversification of the aboriginal communities themselves.

. what i have tried to do here is touch on the key events of the last 40 years with an emphasis on the indigenous basis of these events.

the 60s: a historical turning point
in indian country, the 60s was a time when sea changes led to crises and conflict, and ultimately a new paradigm in indian-government relations. the changes that had been made to the indian act in 1951, while leaving much of the colonial mechanisms in place, had removed the worst restrictions on status indians. importantly, they were free to move from reserves without needing indian agent permission and this, with other demographic changes, led to a substantial migration to urban areas. the perceived "indian problem" in canada became a more visible one. at the same time, aboriginal political activists of earlier decades—fred loft, andrew paull, malcolm norris, john tootoosis, jules sioui—had laid the groundwork for a new generation of dissident political leaders who were prepared to take a more confrontational approach with government. the 1951 indian act had also removed the ban that had existed since 1927 on raising funds to support first

nations' claims or grievances and that also contributed to the dynamic that reached fruition in the 60s.

the federal government knew that its existing policies were not working. they had hired an academic, harry hawthorne, to conduct a national level survey of indian peoples. his widely discussed report made a strong case for change by making it clear that indians were at the bottom of the socio-economic scale in canada.

in the late 60s the new trudeau government, inspired in part by the civil rights movement in the u.s. (and never appreciating that the structural position of african-americans in their struggle for equality was quite different than that of aboriginal canadians in their struggle to protect their cultures), proposed a drastic policy shift. at its core was removal of aboriginal rights. developed under the leadership of then indian affairs minister jean chrétien, the white paper, in which the proposal was made, became a flash point for aboriginal activists. the white paper proposed removing all legal and constitutional markers of aboriginal difference in the interest of promoting equality rights. its practical effect would have been to remove aboriginal rights, the additional rights that aboriginal people had by virtue of being prior occupants of canada.

the struggle over the white paper became a historical turning point. aboriginal leaders united in the cause of having it repudiated, and their opposition proved so successful they were able to force the federal government to withdraw the proposals. although colonialism was still the order of the day, and although no positive policy was developed to replace the white paper, it became the case that a measure of support among aboriginal peoples became seen as necessary for policy initiatives. for just over 100 years policies were developed at the whim of officials; after 1970 aboriginal peoples became major players in policy development. an era of consultation, however insincere, partial and otherwise flawed, had begun.

the 70s: fighting back

the new era did not begin smoothly. aboriginal organizations began to develop, most funded by government but remaining at arm's length. by the mid 70s, different organizations to represent status indians (the national indian brotherhood), non-status indians and métis (the native council of canada), indian women (native women's association of canada) and inuit (the inuit tapirisat of canada) had all formed. all acted to a degree as pressure groups and gave voice to a rising set of demands. these would come to form an institutional layer of the struggle between the state and aboriginal peoples. a further institutional layer came through the courts. two cases i've already mentioned, in 1973 at the supreme court of canada level, were quite important. the calder case involved land rights of the nisga'a nation. did the nisga'a have continuing aboriginal title to their territory? the court determined that aboriginal title was a legal concept. although the nisga'a lost the case on a technicality, it was a victory at a broader level and led to the government restarting the treaty process (called comprehensive land claims at the time). the lavel/bedard cases involved sex discrimination in the indian act through the notorious "out-marriage" provisions (indian women losing their status through marriage to non-indians). the courts rejected the women's claim to equality rights, a rejection supported at the time by the national indian brotherhood. this set the struggle of native women back at least a decade.

meanwhile, communities themselves often took the lead in the policy vacuum as the struggle for aboriginal rights took on local dimensions. a blockade at kenora over racial discrimination and ownership of anishinabe park in the early 70s played a critical role in coalescing the grassroots opposition to colonialism in canada. this led to a cross-canada caravan to ottawa of indian activists with some non-aboriginal supporters. the far left suffered a significant setback in its relations with first nations: at the final confrontation between the new rcmp tactical division and the demonstrators on parliament hill, the indian activists found their "radical" white brothers and sisters had disappeared and left them alone to face the police in a bloody confrontation. i'm told, though, by an activist who was present that this was at a request of aboriginal activists, who wanted to take the lead and be the "front" of the struggle. it is clear that misunderstandings among the aboriginal and non-aboriginal activists led to separation and some acrimony between the groups. this acrimony, along with a general failure of the left to develop strong lines of solidarity with the dynamic "red power" movement led by the likes of vern harper and howard adams, meant a significant lost opportunity for socialism to establish a strong connection with aboriginal activism.

three other significant struggles in the decade involved resource use and illustrated the potential power of aboriginal peoples. in james bay, the québec government's plan to ignore the cree and inuit whose environment would be affected by proposed hydroelectric development was quickly scuttled: the first modern treaty, involving hundreds of millions of dollars, was eventually negotiated in order to secure aboriginal cooperation. in the northwest territories, dene were successful in preventing the construction of a proposed gas pipeline down the mackenzie valley, in part thanks to the success of the berger inquiry. in northern manitoba, hydroelectric development projects went ahead, though a northern flood agreement (nfa) there, effectively a modern treaty, promised in part "the alleviation of poverty" for the affected communities. the subsequent outright betrayal of the nfa and manitoba hydro's largely successful attempt to buy its way out of that deal (only one community of the original five, pimicikamak, continues to refuse a buyout package) is an unfortunate example of the state duplicity that ultimately affected each of the three regional struggles. a smaller scale pipeline was built in the mackenzie valley in the mid 80s, below the media horizon, and the james bay cree quickly realized their land claim would not be implemented with the spirit of generosity that had informed negotiations.

the 80s: from constitutional negotiations
to grassroots resistances

by the late 70s, attention turned from grassroots-led initiatives to the struggle over the proposed constitution. aboriginal leaders recognized that repatriating the constitution in a sense "raised the stakes" around the issue of aboriginal rights: they would be included and secured, or excluded and likely lost. a great deal of energy went into negotiating and lobbying for the eventual inclusion of sections 25, 35, and 37 in the constitution act of 1982. the sections ensured that the charter of rights and freedoms could not be used to limit aboriginal rights (s 25), that aboriginal and treaty rights were recognized and affirmed (s 35), and more meetings would be held to define and identify those rights (s 37). section 25 should be emphasized here because it was a direct result of the fact that seared into the memory of a generation of aboriginal political leaders was the struggle over the white paper, which proposed equality at the expense of aboriginal rights; section 25 said that the equality rights entrenched in the canadian charter of rights would not be interpreted in any way that diminished aboriginal rights. canada, as a result of its peculiar historical struggle, had found a formula regarding recognizing the difference and potential conflict between aboriginal rights and human rights that still today represents an advance over what the united nations has established. in all, these sections represented a significant victory for aboriginal peoples and ensured that a proposal like the white paper could not be reintroduced, though government eventually found other ways to sneak it in. this struggle was at an institutional level involving lawyers and leading politicians. to some extent it led to a bureaucratization of the grassroots movement that had emerged in the 70s.

three outcomes of the institutional struggle in the decade were the 1983 publication of the penner report, a special parliamentary committee report that endorsed the idea of aboriginal self-government as a new paradigm; the passing of bill c-31 in 1985 which reduced sex discrimination in the indian act and established a process whereby individuals who had lost status (and their children) could regain it; and four meetings between aboriginal leaders and the premiers and prime minister between 1983 and 1987 whose purpose was to give greater substance to section 35. the meeting in 1983 did produce a significant amendment to section 35, ensuring that aboriginal and treaty rights were guaranteed equally to male and female persons, which contributed to ensuring that bill c-31 would pass. while the constitutional meetings failed to more broadly identify and define aboriginal rights, and the more far-reaching of the penner report recommendations were not implemented, and the issue of gender discrimination in the allocation of legal status was only effectively deferred for a generation, both the report and the meetings helped generate public support for aboriginal rights.

the failure of the 1987 first ministers meeting was particularly seen as a betrayal by aboriginal leaders because within months of the march conference, mulroney was announcing a new constitutional deal to bring québec into agreement with the constitution, the ill-fated meech lake accord. the passing of bill c-31 was a tangible success. for all its flaws, at least after 1985 indian women who married non-indians no longer lost their status. however, a generation later there is serious concern that the new two-tiered "status" system could lead to demographic erasure of status indians, and that women who regained status

only regained a status their children can hold if they themselves marry a person with status. strikingly, immediately
after the passage of bill c-31, the mulroney government
initiated cutbacks to two programs of critical importance
to the very people regaining status: the off-reserve housing
program was axed, and the funding for aboriginal post-
secondary students was severely restricted.

three particular struggles gained attention in this
decade: the lubicon lake cree (alberta) struggle to have
their land rights recognized, the innu (northern québec
and labrador) struggle to end nato overflights of their
homeland, nitassinan, and the teme-augama anishnabai
struggle (ontario). in each of these struggles civil disobedience helped generate significant media attention and
significant non-aboriginal support among social activists.
here, the record of christians with a social conscience was
as strong as that of the secular left. the outcomes of these
struggles indicated a hardening of the state in the face of
increased resistance. the lubicon won a partial victory that
was almost instantly erased by a state strategy of splitting
the community. the innu victory over low overflights—
government did not build the large flight training facility
it lobbied nato to have—was more due to the fall of the
berlin wall than the success of the very lively protest movement. subsequent events in nitassinan, particularly the
voisey bay nickel deposit discoveries, and new proposals

for hydro development in the region, have generated a new layer of concern for the innu. while at temagami the land ownership case was lost in the courts, they did manage to secure joint management of forestry resources and saved some of the old growth forest in the area.

the 90s: in the shadow of kanesatake

as the decade began, aboriginal people got a measure of revenge on the mulroney regime by playing a role in killing the meech lake accord in june of 1990: elijah harper's opposition in the manitoba legislature alongside that of newfoundland premier wells led to the demise of that backroom deal. within a month, a conflict at kanesatake— known widely as oka—in québec had quickly escalated to the point where a provincial police officer had been killed and the army called in. this captured international media attention and galvanized a remarkable wave of civil dissent in indian country all across canada, as dissidents watched and worried over the face-to-face standoff that unfolded. although the standoff ended relatively peacefully, many of canada's open wounds were exposed to the world: racism towards aboriginal people at mercier bridge; failure of institutional vehicles like the land claim process to deal with legitimate aboriginal land rights; and an emergent new militancy in indian country were all made more apparent.

kanesatake led directly to the creation of a royal commission on aboriginal peoples, a major institutional process that dominated the early half of the decade and resulted in a five-volume, substantial report recommending a drastic change in direction for aboriginal policy. as might have been predicted, the report was almost entirely ignored by government. meanwhile, the other major constitutional proposal developed at charlottetown held more promise for aboriginal peoples than its predecessor. but aboriginal people were as divided as the rest of the country regarding it and many were not sorry to see the proposals fail.

some progress was made in other institutional places. the supreme court of canada attempted to give weight to treaty rights and section 35 of the constitution on two major decisions, sioui and sparrow (both 1990). later in the decade it overturned a racist bc court decision involving the land rights of gitksan and witsuwit'en peoples (the delgamuukw case). the federal government officially changed policy to support an inherent right to aboriginal self-government, a critical stalling point in the constitutional debates of the previous decade, though its vision of self-government remained quite limited at the practical level. the creation of nunavut, a homeland for inuit in the far north with the status of a territorial government, was the most promising development at the institutional level but one based on the unique circumstances of inuit and not a model that could be easily applied elsewhere.

while all of the earlier grassroots conflicts continued to smoulder—the james bay cree, in particular, taking an increasingly visible role in opposition to further proposed export-based hydroelectric development in their territories—new local level crises developed. a conflict in southern alberta on the oldman river did not generate extensive media attention but pointed to the continued disjuncture between "development" planners and first nations. at stoney point in ontario, a peaceful occupation of state-expropriated reserve lands led to the murder of dudley george, one of the aboriginal activists. and in gustavson lake, bc, an attempt to reclaim traditional spiritual lands quickly escalated into a police blockade and near violence. interestingly, the media tended to stay away from these conflicts: having devoted significant attention to kanesatake and the earlier struggles, it is as if it decided only death was enough to generate its sustained attention.

the decade ended with one promising development— a land claim settlement for the nisga'a nation. the nisga'a had been responsible for restarting the modern treaty process through the calder case. but the province of bc had consistently blocked attempts to settle their claim by not freeing up so-called provincial crown land. a combination of a change in the provincial position spearheaded by the ndp, and significant changes in the federal government's land claims policy in the aftermath of kanesatake, but most importantly a decade of grassroots activism from haida gwai to the southern interior, led to the beginning of a flawed but better than non-existent treaty process still underway in bc in spite of occasional provincial government attempts to stop it. while only two comprehensive claims had been settled in the 70s and 80s five, including the nisga'a, were settled in the 90s. the land claims policy remains focused on establishing "certainty" of land ownership and each new claim can be said to be a page in the last chapter of the conquest of the americas that dispossesses aboriginal peoples of their traditional territories. but at least the first nations can be comforted by the fact that they have a few more negotiating options.

new millennium, ancient story
the first few years of a decade i call the "nothings" saw a significant backpedalling on the meagre gains that have been made. a supreme court decision regarding micmaw fishing rights, along with micmaw attempts to assert those rights, led to an unprecedented court "clarification" of its decision and a nasty fight on the maritime waters, particularly at burnt church, where significant issues remain unresolved. in 2003 a lower court in bc attempted to reverse the sparrow decision on fishing rights there. apparently

you can overturn judicial hierarchy when it comes to aboriginal issues. the james bay cree signed a 3.5 billion dollar agreement with the québec government (70 million dollars in each of 50 years). though the community most affected by hydro development, chisasibi, remarkably showed great courage by voting narrowly against the deal, the other communities supported it enough that it passed. at grassy narrows, ontario, a fire was lit in december of 2002 and a blockade set up to protest clear-cut logging in the area. the peacefulness and reasonableness of the demonstrators has meant a virtual media blackout on the blockade, which became the longest running blockade in canadian history.

the state also prepared its first major rewrite to the indian act in a half century (the only important changes in the period being those in the mid 80s referred to above). the first nations governance act was effectively a colonial repetition. in the 1880s the state imposed the band council electoral system (in some places forcibly) to "teach the indians about democracy." in 2003 the government condemned the band council electoral system it invented and tried unsuccessfully to impose a newer vision of "teaching the indians about democracy." strikingly, the lead-up to this legislation involved systematically discrediting the first nations leadership so their opposition would be muted, effectively turning history back to a pre white paper regime of making change with only the most meagre pretense of consultation. but serious opposition from first nations eventually scuttled an act that the minister has promised "would be" implemented: not the first or last time the state's agenda was derailed by grassroots opposition.

later in the decade, the ontario government made a very strong effort to ignore the results of its "consultations" with the kitchenuhmaykoosib inninuwug in its far northwest. when the chief and council tried to say "no means no" to a proposed platinum mine in their traditional territory, they were summarily arrested at the order of a lower court judge. the outcry over this led to a massive movement in support of the first nations leaders and generated a sustained support movement among settler-newcomers. the leaders were eventually freed on orders of superior court, and successfully prevented the mine development, while the movement of support led to strong urban based non-aboriginal allies around aboriginal rights issues. this has led to significant made-in-canada resistance, led by aboriginal communities, to development of the tar sands. in toronto, the long-simmering dispute over caledonia land issues has led to a strong support movement there. against these developments the harper regime moved, initially somewhat quietly though growing increasingly bellicose, to privatize reserve lands and discredit various aboriginal leaders. this in turn has led to a massive outcry—the idle no more movement—sparked by women in saskatchewan and the courageous hunger strike of chief theresa spence.

in 1963, canada was characterized in part by a colonial regime within its borders. in 2013 the colonial regime remains in place, though a determined and multi-faceted struggle has won some significant victories by using the tool of aboriginal or treaty rights. in 1963 many canadians would view an aboriginal ancestor as a skeleton in the closet to be somewhat ashamed of, but now many canadians scour their closets in an effort to find an aboriginal ancestor they can claim as their own. at the level of expressive cultural politics, there has been a shift towards appropriating instead of excluding aboriginal culture, for better or worse. on the ground, as the last parcels of aboriginal title are surrendered and the conquest completed—something that will likely happen in our lifetime—and as canadian energy resources in aboriginal homelands become increasingly critical to capital accumulation, aboriginal peoples are very likely to continue to live on a marginal front line of the anti-capitalist struggle, using treaty or aboriginal rights as a significant lever to protect their lands and sovereignty.

ii. inuit country

what follows deals in an introductory way with a specific group of indigenous people in canada, the inuit. inuit are indigenous occupants of the arctic in canada, the u.s., russia and greenland. they have a distinct land base, distinct legal status, distinct culture, and distinct colonial history; yet the notion of aboriginal rights remains clearly relevant. in the united states they are still referred to as eskimos (which does not mean "eaters of raw meat" as is commonly thought; the derivation of "eskimo" remains disputed), and as a result that word still has global currency, though canada and denmark have both replaced the word with "inuit," a self-designation meaning "people." geographically, in canada inuit occupy the northernmost regions (beyond the tree line) in the northwest territories, nunavut, labrador, and northern québec. culturally, inuit are hunting peoples whose traditional life was built almost entirely around snow, bone, skin, and ice. for archaeologists, inuit are descendants of a migration across the bering strait that took place about 1,000 years ago, whereas in their view most indigenous americans are likely descended from people who migrated 10 to 12 thousand years ago. inuit traditionally have been gatherers and hunters, like many other indigenous peoples, but have their own distinct cultural expressions of this embodied in stories, games, artworks, tools, clothing, and so on that are immediately recognizable and, indeed, famous.

historically, inuit engagement with colonial capitalism has also been distinct. in canada, although early contact with inuit took place in the 16th century, sustained contacts did not happen until the mid and late 19th century, with the search for the franklin expedition and the arctic whale hunt being the major drivers of the process. missionary activity in arctic canada becomes a sustained force at this time, and by the early 20th century a fox fur trade became important. the canadian state's involvement in the arctic was sporadic and fitful until the postwar period; in the late 1950s a policy of neglect transformed dramatically as the welfare state moved to take control of many aspects of inuit people's lives. the indian act has only very briefly regulated inuit. hence, to this day, inuit communities do not have the chief and council structure that first nations deal with, there are no inuit reserves, and inuit have not had to deal with the vexing problem of legal "status." however, inuit are constitutionally recognized as indigenous peoples with aboriginal rights. inuit never signed historic treaties, but have been leaders in negotiating comprehensive land claims or modern treaties.

it is important to stress that in modern times no event has had as devastating an impact on inuit communities as the animal rights/greenpeace-sponsored boycott of seal fur products from the early 70s. communities that had been self-sustaining became dependent in large measure on government handouts, because seal fur prices plummeted. it is still the case that the one most significant activity canadians who support inuit can engage in is buying inuit-produced sealskin products, thereby allowing hunters to support a land-based lifestyle. no mine or energy project would ever be as valuable to inuit as a renewed market for sealskin (see george wenzel's *animal rights human rights* or hugh brody's *living arctic* on this question).

politically, inuit are represented internationally by the in-uit circumpolar conference, nationally in canada by the inuit tapiriit kanatami, and in the separate provinces and territories by land claims-based groups, such as the inuvialuit regional corporation in the beaufort sea area of the nwt, or makivik in northern québec. in canada an inuit women's organiza-tion, pauktuutit, represents inuit women from all the regions. inuit have been involved in struggles that parallel those of first nations and métis in other parts of canada, struggles over resource development/destruction, to assert land title, to achieve self-determination and self-government, and to defend inuit aboriginal rights. although in greenland a strong socialist movement exists among inuit, socialism among inuit in canada has not been able to establish itself in any sustained way. similarly, the various inuit struggles have not generated the kind of non-aboriginal support activities or drawn upon civil disobedience actions that other indigenous activist com-munities have sometimes engaged.

yet, inuit have a remarkable history of resistance to the canadian state and in one part of arctic canada have established a public government and territory that they democratically control: nunavut. from the time of the first inuit land-based petition to the government (1953) to the early 70s when inuit first established a national political body (then called the inuit tapirisat of canada, now itk), inuit have been a quick study in responding to colonial capitalism. inuit have also been leaders in developing language retention for their language (inuktitut) and have produced remarkable and dynamic contemporary cultural and artistic expressions from prints, sculpture, and stories, to film and music.

a socialism informed about inuit issues may become a socialism of relevance to inuit; inuit may themselves offer many resources to a broader socialist project to build a better world.

a great deal of material can be found in books, online, and through films about inuit. i have to recommend the works frank tester and i have coauthored, *tammarniit (mistakes)* and *kiumajut (talking back),* as histories that focus on state-sponsored colonialism in the 50s and 60s. hugh brody's work, *the people's land* and *the other side of eden,* offers a strong discussion of inuit hunting cultures in a modern frame. the zacharias kunuk/norman cohn films *atanarjuat* and *the journals of knut rasmussen* are enormously exciting and rewarding dramatic pieces that immerse viewers in an inuit world view.

a struggle continues to unfold in the regions of the arctic claimed by canada. stephen harper's conservatives want to spend enormous resources militarizing the area in the name of canadian sovereignty. mary simon, among other inuit leaders, has pointed out that instead of icebreakers, arctic military exercises, and warplanes, a government that worked with arctic occupants, the inuit, would surely offer the strongest reason for inuit themselves to want to be in canada and therefore protect its arctic interests. alongside of this, rapacious colonial capitalism, which harperites also cheerlead for, desires the energy and mineral resources that can be found in abundance under arctic lands and waters. while hunting continues to thrive among inuit, these new mega resource projects pose a serious challenge to inuit and now often come with some degree of inuit "leadership" support. the issues are even more complex given the enormous social problems "modernization" has created, including youth suicide rates among the highest in the world. inuit therefore continue to pose a challenge, by their very existence, to the canadian national project: will it be founded on a rapacious capitalism for which "development" is defined solely as the growth of capital, or will it be founded on the development of our human capacities, our appreciation and admiration for the contributions inuit culture has to offer to humanity, and our respect for a justice that deserves the name?

iii. the violence of the letter:
land claims and the continuing colonial conquest

the recent struggle over lands in southern ontario near caledonia, mentioned earlier, points to the continuing problem with land claims policy in canada. this sentence could be used to begin an article every few years; only the place names change: the recent struggle at grassy narrows, the recent struggle at stoney point, the recent struggle at oka. while there is a sense in which the current land claims policy goes back to the beginnings of colonialism in canada, the recent permutations are worth attention. any understanding of contemporary conflicts needs to be informed by a strong and detailed sense of what has happened historically, as well as what is happening today. one of the key elements of aboriginal rights, called aboriginal title, is the foundation of this struggle.

a brief history of aboriginal title

aboriginal people insist that their land ownership comes from their having lived upon and used the land since "when the world was new" (to use dene elder george blondin's phrase). the canadian state says that aboriginal title derives from a set of legal documents like the royal proclamation of 1763. guess who holds all the cards, and whose view gets the most attention? however, the doctrine of prior occupancy has been enshrined as the source of aboriginal title and rights, so perhaps the state doesn't always get its way.

the royal proclamation of 1763 was a founding constitutional document for canada. after the seven years war, the british needed to remove the military regimes that ran what was then new france and the other newly won british possessions. in october, 1763, a proclamation was printed that established civilian governors in each of the new british "possessions"; but about half of the document dealt with aboriginal land issues. fearing another rebellion in the wake of pontiac's attempts to drive the invaders back across the ocean, the government decided on a policy of appeasement with aboriginal peoples and promised to respect their land rights. to do that, the proclamation stated that only the crown, not private citizens or colonial governors, could buy land from "indians," and must do so for a fair price and in a public process.

what are called the "historic" treaties were based on this. in 1850 william robinson negotiated two treaties around lake huron and lake superior and these became the model for treaty-making in the 19th century. when canada "purchased" rupert's land from the hudson's bay company in 1869 it had unfinished business, since the real landowners were first nations and métis. métis land rights were negotiated through a process of providing individual scrip (though, since there came to be a great deal of fraud associated with the process, it was really an unsuccessful effort to extinguish métis title). first nations were dealt with collectively through treaty negotiations. treaties 1 through 7 were negotiated between 1871 and 1877 by alexander morris. these are sometimes called the "southern" numbered treaties and did involve some negotiations and concessions on the part of the state. The "northern" numbered treaties, from 1899 to 1921 or treaty 8 to treaty 11, involved government negotiators with a document they themselves had no power to change: first nations were simply supposed to sign on the dotted lines. there was likely some chicanery in this process as well as in the process of getting some first nations to sign "adhesions" to earlier treaties. the historic treaties are only a few pages in length, and involve vague promises of support in exchange for apparently clear surrender of aboriginal title to lands (not waters!). however, the first nations who signed them are right to suggest that if the spirit of the treaties were properly respected they would be much more valuable. hence the ongoing struggle for treaty rights in canada.

the first of the modern treaties was the james bay and northern québec agreement of the mid 70s, negotiated at the height of, and in order to resolve, the conflict around hydroelectric development in northern québec. subsequent deals were slow in coming. the western arctic agreement with inuvialuit in the northwest territories in the mid 80s was next. eventually the nunavut agreement was signed, several dene and métis groups in the nwt signed agreements in the 90s, as did several of the first nations in the yukon. in the latter part of the 90s and early part of the nothings, the nisga'a and tli'chon in bc and the nwt signed complex modern treaties that included strong self-government arrangements, though many observers thought the concessions they agreed to were also too strong.

in all of these historic and contemporary agreements the core government demand was the surrender or "extinguishment" of aboriginal title. the language of these agreements is extraordinarily ruthless. for example, the much-lauded nunavut claim says in part, "inuit hereby cede, release and surrender to her majesty the queen in right of canada, all their aboriginal claims, rights, title and interests, if any, in and to lands and waters anywhere within canada." similar language exists in each of the treaties and each of the modern treaties.

only two agreements, the recent tli'chon (dene) and the nisga'a agreements, do not have an extinguishment clause but rather a clause stating that the text of those claims specify all the aboriginal rights of the respective first nations. i call this the "exhaustion" model because it says the treaties fully "exhaust" aboriginal rights and title. none exist outside the agreement. in some ways, this is even more totalizing or all-encompassing than the extinguishment clause. trust the federal government, after decades of criticism over extinguishment as the basis of their policy, to come up with something worse!

counter-tactics
aboriginal peoples have responded with a variety of tactics. some, like the nisga'a, have been extremely patient, knowing that they will still be there when another generation of bureaucrats and policies come along, and taking the opportunity when it comes to negotiate a creative model. inuit, frustrated at the unwillingness of the government to include self-government provisions in their land claim, opted for a public government model through the creation of nunavut as a way out of that impasse.

first nations have been able to take the "one size fits all" approach of the federal government and pretty much tear it to shreds. the yukon, nunavut, nisga'a, tli'chon and other nwt dene/métis claims all look quite different from one another. and, when the government "deals with" a land claim by rejecting it, many first nations have been willing to take actions into their own hands, asserting their just sense of ownership over their traditional territories through blockades or occupations.

on the treaty-rights front, i recently attended a meeting at opaskwayak cree nation in northern manitoba, where there was much evidence that "enough is enough" when it comes to erosion of treaty rights. intense frustration with the lack of respect for treaty rights is currently leading to a grassroots, treaty-based alliance on the prairies, outside of existing political structures, in order to push for stronger recognition of treaties.

continuing the conquest

so, what is all this about? if the government is prepared to negotiate, giving big chunks of money to first nations in exchange for them surrendering their land, where's the complaint? simply put, most first nations see modern treaties as ways of reaffirming and asserting their continuing ownership of their traditional territories. the state sees modern treaties as a way of ending that ownership in "exchange" for much smaller pieces of land and a small chunk of capital. this is called "certainty," and it is the state's stated goal. and why is certainty required? because our old friend capital, private interest, needs certainty in order to "invest," in order to continue to tear up the land at its unsustainable pace. yes, capital accumulation lurks in the wings, and here the state fully acts as its representative. this, then, is "about" the conquest, that centuries-old process of dispossessing native americans in order to allow others to accumulate wealth. while in spanish times the conquest took the form of murder and physical genocide,

in our colder, politer nation and times the conquest takes
the form of the "violence of the letter": documents signed
in backrooms by judges and negotiators and politicians,
carrots on sticks that help enable elite aboriginal leaders
to manage the capital resources of their peoples by tying
them to further destruction of their own lands (only now
as investors). as i noted earlier, marx called this exact process "primitive accumulation." i myself also like to call it
the "racial reconfiguration and redistribution of wealth"
because it involves taking the wealth of gatherers and
hunters—their self-sustaining land-based economy, their
leisure time, their communities—away from them and
reconfiguring it to "resources" as capital, then "redistrib-
uting" that wealth to the south. since so often in the world
this process crosses a racial boundary, i think it is useful
to think of it as a racial reconfiguration and redistribution
of wealth. another way to think this is that the wealth of
a hunting mode of production must be transformed into
the wealth recognizable by capitalism and then, basically,
it can be stolen from first peoples. aboriginal rights, and
aboriginal title as critical among them, becomes a mechanism for fighting this global process.

the word "perfidy," used by none other than johnny
cash to describe the way treaties were respected in the
united states on his never-surpassed album, *bitter tears*,
does not only apply to 19th century dealings, but goes

straight to the heart of what has been happening in canada in the last few decades.

for example, while the inuvialuit in the western arctic were negotiating their claim in the early 80s, the federal government insisted that offshore resources were not under consideration. period. the so-called "pragmatic" in-uvialuit leaders decided they couldn't change such a policy and, even though they sat adjacent to one of the largest oil and gas reserves in canada (offshore in the beaufort sea), they settled a claim without gaining access to any of those reserves. having got their agreement, when it came time to review policy a few years later, the canadian government could then put offshore resources back on the table for those few other indigenous people without previous treaty agreements who might take small advantage of it.

in the sahtu region, the government negotiated a land claim separate from a self-government agreement. it also in-sisted that corporate structures be set up to administer the land claim separate from the existing band council struc-tures. this has effectively led to a dual power structure in the region, with under-resourced band councils having to go hat in hand to local land claims corporations for funding. and as a mackenzie gas project started to work its way down the val-ley, key communities in its path have a split leadership, two groups to negotiate with one another, as well as outsiders, which obviously weakens their bargaining power.

will the federal government negotiate self-government there to ease and clarify the situation, in spite of the fact that the sahtu treaty itself says they "shall" do so at the request of the communities? only with those communities willing to play their game and settle for self-government in the narrowest terms, as a matter of administrating programs and services. it will not, it appears, negotiate with fort good hope, the key community on the projected pipeline's path in the northern part of the region, which in february 2006 voted against a draft impacts and benefit agreement offered by imperial oil (not something that the pipeline-boosting *globe and mail* would ever consider reporting).

quite some time ago, none other than karl marx (yes, him!) emphasized that the critical levers in the historical development of capitalism are "those moments when great masses of men are suddenly and forcefully torn from their means of subsistence" (*capital* 876). this, i again stress, is at the core of what he called "primitive accumulation" (with few taking note of the fact that marx uses anthropological language against european modernism, a revolutionary textual strategy).

in northern canada though, it is the very means of subsistence, the land base, which remains capital and the state's great incentive; to them, a few more impoverished first nations are simply a happy by-product. and this is what is happening in canada, a legacy of our oldest, most unjust, ineffective, unethical, unconscionable policy: land claims. the conquest is not a matter of ancient or even recent history: we, our generation, are carrying on the work of the conquest today. it is the core principle coded into the word "certainty" (and its two flunkies, "extinguishment" and "exhaustion") that is the basis of an approach to land claims that is still with us.

iv. towards a new policy paradigm for first peoples

the current policy paradigm surrounding aboriginal issues is locked within a very narrow compass of possibility. the two major ideas that emerged in the last decade were the proposals around the governance act, rejected by most first nations leaders, and the kelowna accord, endorsed by the assembly of first nations, but dead in the water thanks to the current harper regime. the former involved imposing a one-size-fits-all governance model onto first nations; the latter involved providing much-needed resources for infrastructure and social programs. neither proposal involved a change to the current policy paradigm.

for the party of the right, that paradigm involves mouthing grudging respect for aboriginal rights without actually treating them seriously, together with more resources for band-aid solutions, with "modernization," "progress," and "advancement" the buzzwords. for the party of the far right, the paradigm involves ignoring or suppressing aboriginal rights, reducing the resources offered for band-aid solutions, even more bombastically intoning the same set of buzzwords and, more recently, intoning the mantra of privatization while interfering with any local elected first nations leaders who disagree.

here are some ideas for genuinely progressive change to the current paradigm.

take aboriginal rights seriously

start from the presumption that aboriginal and treaty rights are the foundation of policy. this means taking the supreme court of canada at its word, developing a "liberal and generous" approach to aboriginal and treaty rights. it means honouring and respecting the cultural distinctiveness of aboriginal peoples and paying close attention to oral histories and oral understandings. these are not mere slogans. if turned into serious policy, it would mean developing frameworks whose basic goal is not to "modernize," but rather to support and invigorate traditional cultural forms in a contemporary context. what follows offers some substantive ways of moving in this direction.

remove colonial power structures

replace the indian act with a first peoples' governance recognition act, which would empower local aboriginal authorities with province-like responsibilities (in early 1984 the trudeau cabinet killed a proposal for a first nations recognition and validation act, which would have worked in a similar fashion). determination of so-called "indian status" would be turned over to those authorities. this governance recognition act would not mandate the form of first peoples' governing institutions; it would simply have the function of recognizing the systems developed by aboriginal communities and developing appropriate institutional linkages to the broader polity.

provide a new basis for financial support
develop a specific revenue stream that draws off a portion of resource royalties or taxes from non-renewable resource development on traditional lands. a portion of this stream could go directly to the local aboriginal communities affected by such developments, and a portion to a general fund for improvement of aboriginal communities' social and physical infrastructures. aboriginal communities should enjoy the same infrastructural amenities as non-aboriginal communities, and the way to achieve that is not to relocate them, or every five years develop a new housing program. the way to achieve it is to provide an ongoing financial base.

share the land
develop joint-management arrangements with all rural and remote aboriginal communities for the traditional

land base of the first peoples involved. such plans should recognize and strongly support those communities that wish to keep the hunting economy as a base of well-being by deploying strong environmental protection measures. both social and material infrastructures can be developed in ways that would support well-being in the context of a contemporary hunting economy. those communities prepared to support non-renewable resource development must have a role in planning (and finding environmental mitigations) and establishing direct benefits from such development.

remove "certainty," whether through the former extinguishment model or the current exhaustion model, as the basis of modern treaties. instead, develop treaties that do not surrender or exhaust aboriginal rights and title, but rather affirm them. the treaties would amount to versions of the joint-management arrangements discussed above, and specific revenue-sharing or resource-sharing provisions appropriate to the first peoples involved.

encourage urban communities
allow for the creation of legal community structures (now called bands) and governance bodies in urban contexts and among groups of aboriginal peoples including so-called "non-status indians" and others who may have indian but not band status, or who do not have band affiliation. such

communities within the broader community would pro-
mote cultural distinctiveness in an urban context. urban
"reserves" could also be used as a structure for housing rather
than merely commercial outlets as in the current paradigm.

develop culturally based social programs
the delivery of healthcare, education, social assistance,
child and family services, and justice should all be under
the authority of first peoples' governance structures, and
funded on a block-transfer basis similar to provincial
authorities. creative alternatives to the existing delivery
models, based on the traditions and values of the specific
community, should be encouraged. in particular, in the far
and mid north, land-based healing and justice programs
need to be expanded. traditional language and knowledge
holders should be recognized and given strong roles in
education. land-based education should be emphasized.
social assistance and material support should be provided
to land-based families. renewable resource officers should
not be university-trained non-aboriginal peoples, but
traditional hunting, trapping, and fishing families. a
policy trajectory that puts people out on the land and
supports them with equipment and other resources
would reverse more than a century of policies that do
the opposite, and would support the traditional mode of
production.

one simple starting point would be to mandate the
justice department to ensure that all laws passed by parliament pass a test to ensure they substantively respect
aboriginal and treaty rights. revoking the recent omnibus
bill that reduces environmental protection and promotes
privatization of reserve lands would be another excellent
beginning. a particular mechanism for ensuring aboriginal
presence in cabinet, parliament, and senate could also be
developed: a special set of parliamentary seats, reserved
seats in senate, a consultation panel for the supreme court,
and a special cabinet level consultation group would all be
viable ideas. a more far-reaching approach might look to
consolidate certain parts of the provincial north in québec,
ontario, and manitoba as a province.

there is much more that needs to be done—and
urgently—but this outlines what a set of policies based on
a substantive application of aboriginal and treaty rights
might look like. the overall principles are in place through
the legal framework developed in the last two decades by
the supreme court of canada. but political leaders have
neither the understanding nor the political will to move
in anything like this direction.

governments of the right and the far right have alike
done all in their power to ignore, confine, limit, and foot-
drag on the principles enunciated as constitutional law
by our courts. perhaps we should be much more direct

with the ruling elites of our time, and simply demand of them that, in the area of policy-making with respect to first peoples, they obey the law.

v. turning the page on colonial oppression: defenders of the land and idle no more!

early in the fall of 2009, an event largely ignored by the mass media in canada took place in northwestern ontario. a float plane filled with equipment and staff from the plat-inex mining company attempted to land on big trout lake, known as kitchenuhmaykoosib to the local inninuwug. the chief and other members of the community got in their boats and played a game of "chicken" with the plane, maneuvering their boats in front of its landing trajectory to keep it from being able settle onto the lake. after making several attempts, the pilot turned around and returned south. a few months later the community heard the news that the ontario government had bought out platinex's interest in the disputed territory (part of treaty 9) and announced that the platinum mining development in the region would not proceed.

i heard about the story from sam mckay at a defenders of the land gathering that fall in vancouver. he was one of six members of the kitchenuhmaykoosib inninuwug band council jailed for trying to fight off platinex a year and a half earlier. this provisional victory, along with a few others—charges were dropped in the fall against grassy narrows citizen roberta keesig for building an unlicensed cabin in her family's traditional trapping territory—bolster the spirits of activists trying to turn back the tide of colonialism. colonialism continues to ravage first nations, inuit, and métis lands from real estate, logging, and hydro developments in the west coast, to the tar sands developments in miskew cree and chipewyan territories, to hydro developments in pimicikamak inninew lands north of lake winnipeg, to logging in asubpeeschoseewagong territory in treaty 3, to "development" and government interference in barrier lake, to continued fishing and logging disputes involving mi'kmaq lands and waters on the east coast.

but perhaps nothing is as inspiring as seeing and hearing people from all these communities—and more—gathered together to tell their stories and try to find ways of supporting each other.

gathering together
from november 26 to november 29 in 2009 some of the leading indigenous activists in canada gathered at the ukrainian cultural centre in vancouver. the defenders of the land gathering followed from a similar historic event that took place a year earlier in winnipeg. among those who attended were shuswap's renowned activist arthur manuel, russell diabo (a mohawk from kahnawake now

working with the barrier lake algonquin resistance), sam mckay of kitchenuhmaykoosib inninuwug, mireille lapointe of ardoch algonquin first nation, terry sappier of the maliseet nation resistance, elder irene billy of secwenep opposition to sun peaks development, david etchinelle of shuhtagotine in denendeh, bertha wilson of tsawwassen first nation, delbert guerin of musqueam, eugenie mercredi of pimicikamak, judy dasilva of asubpeeschoseewagong, and mike mercredi of fort chipewyan. the list, a who's who of canadian indigenous activists in attendance at the gathering, is too long to complete here. as mireille lapointe put it, "it's just inspiring to be in this room with these people. it gives me hope. it fills my spirit." manuel and diabo were perhaps the founding activists of the wider group, certainly among its leading and guiding voices.

building on courage
in opening the meeting and welcoming us all to his home, unceded territory, delbert guerin (musqueam) spoke strongly of the courage that was required to stand up and fight back: a courage that had led him as chief to take his nation's case for redress of a land swindle to the supreme court of canada, leading to the famous guerin decision. the defenders of the land gathering was trying to build on the courage of the many activists who were there in at least two ways.

on the one hand, since the mainstream indigenous political organizations have to varying degrees been institutionalized and have a muted role in the actual struggles taking place, it's thought that a different kind of organization is needed, one that comes from the dissident communities, the communities engaged in direct, non-violent opposition to the state. if some kind of a network or vehicle can be created to coordinate these differing oppositions, it is quite possible that a page in canadian history can be turned: something new may happen in the struggle for treaty and aboriginal rights.

on the other hand, there is also a sense that, for perhaps the first time, it may be possible to build a sustained mass movement in support of indigenous struggles in canada. a number of non-indigenous activists, myself included, from the growing number of indigenous peoples solidarity organizations that are springing up were there for that purpose. of some critical significance as well, activists from anti-racist groups like no one is illegal added their voices and learned from the core indigenous speakers.

we shared stories. we workshopped plans. we drafted manifestos and resolutions. we talked and we listened. there was much to be learned from the various battles being fought across canada in indian country. for example, on the flawed tsawwassen treaty process, bertha wilson spoke with passionate anger: "our people who live here, our voices were drowned by all the votes of the people who married out and moved away long ago. they were tempted by the thought of money. they didn't care about the land anymore. we who live here, we have to see what happens to the land. we care about it."

people spoke about the band councils that were fighting back, and about the band councils that were colluding with the state. people spoke about the beauty of traditional territories and the ravages of industrial pollution. there was a shared sense of frustration and anger, and at the same time a determination and resolute hope.

there were real questions to be discussed: for example, how much criticism of mainstream organizations was appropriate? what sort of attention should be devoted to social issues and spirituality? how could this group say and do something about the issue of missing indigenous women? among these, at least one workshop devoted to international forums was led by arthur manuel, who said, "we need to be engaging in this struggle on all levels, from the grassroots to the biggest international organizations. our stories are being heard in geneva and in other centres of international human rights." these issues were discussed in plenary sessions, in workshops, and, often most passionately and pointedly, in small groups sitting around the table and networking during breaks.

defenders of the land will continue, because...

in the non-indigenous peoples' caucus, i learned something about why it's easier to build a support movement for places far away from canada (chile, nicaragua, south africa) than to build one for indigenous movements in canada. it's because in canada we have to forge a real relation with real people. we have to watch our words more closely and accountably. we have to stand aside and let the indigenous leaders do the talking, and we have to ethically confront ourselves in a way that supporting people far away does not demand. this is not to say that other international solidarity work is easy, but rather to point to the specific challenges we face in building a mass movement of support for struggles over aboriginal and treaty rights taking place inside canada. the participation of activists from no one is illegal, anti-racist, and diasporic communities was a significant and welcome part of the gathering in part for this reason.

defenders of the land will continue, because it has to. if artists and academics and, especially, trade unionists in canada can see their way to providing support, it could become the mass movement canada desperately needs. defenders of the land will continue because a justice that deserves the name does not come from corporate "sponsors" or state commissions or enlightened philanthropists or the march of progress, but from the ground up, from the people who directly and daily confront injustice. their willingness to confront the established order, to stand their ground, to say "enough is enough," is, in canada, the space of real hope. defenders of the land will continue because this world, these lands, our country, cannot bear the burden of rapacious greed that motivates the small corps of elite bureaucrats who manage the selling of bush country with the smug self-importance of toadies everywhere. but more importantly, the courage and determination and creativity of the leaders, the real leaders, who came out holds a promise that a page in canadian history, a page called the conquest, a page that still reads in lines of lands taken for profit, this page can perhaps finally be turned.

for idle no more

even more recently and directly as a result of provocative actions by the harper government, a movement inspired and led by aboriginal women has mobilized an extraordinary outburst of mass activity in support of aboriginal and treaty rights. the four saskatchewan women who inspired and founded the movement—nina wilson, sylvia mcadam, jessica gordon, and sheelah mclean—showed a strong understanding and respect for treaty rights and for aboriginal people's land rights. at nearly the same time, chief theresa spence of attawapiskat first nation in northern ontario, began an eventual 44-day hunger strike to call attention to the urgency of the issues that aboriginal communities face in canada. the support and attention they garnered and generated washed like a giant wave over the body politic in canada. idle no more events took place in urban centres and rural communities, in nominally "private" shopping malls and in large open public spaces. large crowds danced to the sound of traditional drums, for brief periods slowing the "business as usual" traffic of commodities and people. the protests were simultaneously celebrations of aboriginal expressive culture in places where it was previously unheard or unwelcome. while in my view the movement's goals were initially somewhat loosely defined and the organizational structure deliberately kept to a minimum, the outpouring of support it generated was impressive, speaking to a wide hunger for the kind of leadership shown by chief spence and the creative tactics promoted by the four founders.

it is certainly striking that this movement is led by women, and that so many aboriginal women are leaders among the defenders of the land. it appears that aboriginal women, who for years were excluded from the official institutional governance structures in their communities and who were largely barred from the table at constitutional negotiations in the 80s and 90s, have put their courage, creativity, and determination to the test by standing up to challenge the status quo. idle no more and the defenders of the land: two sides of the same coin in the currency of struggle against a totalizing state.

part three: damned on this earth

in this part of the book i use some examples drawn from
the struggle of first nations in my own backyard, as it were,
northern manitoba, to try to illustrate why and how this
history and these issues matter. the first chapter, "flooded
and forgotten," provides an overview of the history of manitoba hydro and first nations. it is followed by a chapter
called "the wolf has begun to howl" on an occupation led
by then mayor robbie buck from the municipality of grand
rapids and then chief ovide mercredi from the neighbour-
ing first nation, misipawistik. "how to build a legacy of
hatred," the third chapter, deals with the wuskwatim hydro
project and its "partnership agreement" with the nearby
community of nisichawayasihk/nelson house. a fourth
chapter, "as long as the money flows…," deals with a recent
uprising in the community of tataskweyak/split lake, in the
face of the two latest proposals for hydro projects, keeyask
and conawapa. a very brief note, or fifth chapter, makes a

comment on manitoba hydro's celebration over the new
building it constructed in downtown winnipeg (this was
originally posted as part of an art exhibit on the city of winnipeg by students at the university of winnipeg: april 2007,
with apologies to german scholar walter benjamin who had
something to say about triumphal processions). readers will
quickly see that i have little respect for the approach to first
nations that has characterized manitoba hydro's relations
with them in both the past and the present. respect for traditional life ways (or the hunting mode of production) and
for treaty and aboriginal rights demands a dramatic shift
in the overall policy paradigm which has clearly led to the
immiseration of impacted communities.

i. flooded and forgotten: hydro development
makes a battleground of northern manitoba

as public hearings around enbridge's northern gateway
pipeline begin, national attention is focused more than
ever on the major debates related to tar sands development
in alberta and, increasingly, saskatchewan. quietly slipping
under the public radar, it appears, is another significant set
of energy projects that are not likely to gain major media
time or space: the continued development of hydroelectric
energy in northern manitoba.

travelling up the nelson river, it's easy to see the
impacts of hydro development. the once pristine water

is now silty and not to be trusted for drinking. trees fall into the river everywhere along the shore thanks to erosion caused by constantly fluctuating water levels. ancient graves are being exposed, and sacred sites are now under water. what was once a highway for hunters is now dangerous to travel in winter, as the location of ice pockets created by flooding and retreating water cannot be predicted. a river that was once the basis for life has become deadly.

when the churchill river diversion and lake winnipeg regulation projects were undertaken in the 1970s, national attention was riveted by the mackenzie pipeline project of that era and the struggle against hydro development megaprojects in northern québec. although the communities affected by the churchill river diversion and lake winnipeg regulation projects were sufficiently united and gained enough public support within the province to force a modern treaty on manitoba hydro, known as the northern flood agreement (nfa), the terms of that agreement and the systematic violation of it that ensued over the next decade were no doubt influenced by the low national profile of these projects.

history is about to repeat itself as a new wave of dams is currently under development with equally little media attention. have you heard of the wuskwatim project? or keeyask?

around much of northern manitoba, "hydro" is a dirty word, and for good reason. these previous projects have reconfigured the landscape of the entire region, drying whole rivers and engorging lakes. mercury has likely been released into the groundwater, and wildlife habitat has been destroyed. a once thriving aboriginal fishery on south indian lake was casually destroyed. the footprints and the chair, two of northern manitoba's most spiritually powerful sites, were effectively destroyed. kids from nisichawayasihk get on a bus in the summers and go to the swimming pool in thompson if they want to swim. officials are regularly offered water from the silty river they pronounce as "safe" but refuse to drink from.

manitoba hydro has a racially stratified work force: the highly paid technical and administrative work is done by non-native southerners, and the few jobs that northern cree workers can get continue to be low-paid, menial, and most often temporary.

in the grand rapids hydro facility, as in most others, aboriginal employees push brooms and fill plates for more highly paid engineers from the south. the community is divided between a nearly impoverished first nation and municipality, and a prosperous suburban community built by manitoba hydro for its employees. hydro employees' houses have two electricity meters as their bills are subsidized by the utility, while nearby aboriginal residents are not given any reprieve when their power is cut off due to unpaid bills.

among the cree of northern manitoba, it is clear that the end result of the churchill river diversion and lake winnipeg regulation projects, and the inexpensive hydro rates they have made available to southern manitobans, is ecological and social devastation. it is created by a systematic disregard for aboriginal and treaty rights, and a correlative disdain for the hunting way of life.

the great falls dam, built in 1923, was the first of four on the winnipeg river. it was constructed without any consultation with the first nation most affected by the project (sagkeeng, at that time known as fort alexander), as were the 1960 kelsey generating station on the nelson river and the 1965 grand rapids dam on the saskatchewan river.

the latter project involved the wholesale relocation of the community of chemawawin to easterville. it also completely disrupted the grand rapids first nation (now misipawistik), located at the site of construction, by drying up the site of the once sacred rapids, flooding land, and every year sending more debris into the river and lake, making fishing much more difficult.

by the early 1970s, plans for further major hydro developments were underway, which eventually led to the churchill river diversion and lake winnipeg regulation projects. these projects reshaped the whole hydrology of northern manitoba, to the detriment of six cree communities.

when construction for these projects began, the five first nations affected came together to form the northern flood committee. while they were entirely opposed to the proposed projects, they were eventually forced to concede to a negotiated settlement, the nfa, which allowed development to proceed. like chemawawin, the community of south indian lake was entirely relocated and effectively destroyed as a fishing community due to project-related flooding.

the nfa made many promises. a much-quoted schedule attached to the agreement detailed the promotion of studies for the purpose of the "alleviation of mass poverty and unemployment," which many read as a substantive commitment. however, within a few years it became clear that manitoba hydro, the provincial government, and the federal government were not interested in implementing the agreement in good faith.

rather than creating prosperity for nearby communities, hydro-related flooding has immiserated them. eventually, manitoba hydro planners began to pursue even more dams, but because aboriginal rights were now (since 1982) constitutionally recognized, they needed the cooperation of communities where their actions had created what i call below a legacy of hatred. thus, manitoba hydro

offered each community, separately, a financial settlement for what were called "implementation agreements."
they succeeded in getting four of the five first nations to
sign on, which was sufficient to proceed with a new wave
of projects.

the first dam, wuskwatim, on the burntwood river,
is basically complete, late and significantly over budget.
this project is to be followed by a much larger one, the
keeyask, on the lower nelson river, and then another,
conawapa, also on the nelson river. two other dams, notigi
and gillam island, are on manitoba hydro's wish list. the
power generated by these dams is not needed in manitoba,
but will instead be exported to the united states. interestingly, power sales to the u.s. have slumped as natural gas
exploitation and the economic crises have both led to significantly reduced demand for hydro power. this has led to
a tragedy for nisichawayasihk cree nation, which instead
of seeing revenue pour in from hydro profits is having to
borrow money from its future profits in order to share its
burden of loss. the community meanwhile continues to
have few resources to deal with the endemic social issues
it faces on a daily basis.

after the nfa was signed in the 1970s, the northern flood committee linking communities opposed to
hydro development ceased to exist. the province and
the utility both refused to continue recognizing it and

eventually managed to sideline it and thereby divide the communities.

among the reasons for hydro's continued colonial success is that it now deals with communities one at a time, so opposition is fragmented. however, one of the five nfa signatories, pimicikamak (formerly cross lake), has still not signed an implementation agreement and stands outside hydro's current paradigm, fighting for actual implementation of rights and benefits negotiated through the nfa. they have been enormously creative in their political resistance, developing their own governance system and generally making life difficult by trying to force the utility to live up to its promises. whether they, and the very courageous opposition groups in tataskweyak, nisichawayasihk, and elsewhere, manage to make any gains will depend in part on their story getting a wider hearing in canada and internationally than it has so far.

ii. the wolf has begun to howl:
a report on the camp at grand rapids

ovide has sauntered off to get some ducks. the rest of us sit and chat, idly, nurturing the fire and snacking on bannock. a few jokes are tossed around: mayor robbie buck, a large man with a quick wit, keeps everyone's spirits high. although when we hear shots a few comments about whether the chief has injured himself are tossed around, no one is surprised when he returns with two ducks for two shots. the duck soup i'm eating, it turns out, comes from the chief's catch the day before.

for the past few nights, ovide mercredi, chief of the grand rapids first nation (and, as everyone knows, former national chief of the assembly of first nations) and robbie buck, mayor of the municipality of grand rapids, have been camping on the "spillway." they are camping there to prevent manitoba hydro from alleviating the pressure on its giant water reserves by allowing its spillway dam to open, which would release a huge volume of water onto the dry riverbed. hydro is already running as much water through the generator as it can, so the camp—only a few kilometres off highway 6 at a turnoff about a kilometre before it reaches the community—may create a major headache for them.

the camp is in an area of low brush on what used to be the riverbed of the saskatchewan river. some of the local people, who come out to show support, chat, or bring or eat some food or tea, tell me that this bay was an area where people used to catch fish from shore. it's a welcoming bunch of people, and the place exudes the relaxed pace and friendliness of camp life. they even good-humouredly put up with the red star on my green cuban hat!

the last straw

the spark that lit this fire was a notice sent by hydro via fax, announcing imperiously that the spillway would be opened in two days. earlier in the summer, mayor buck tells me, officials had told locals that the spillway likely wouldn't be opened at all. fishermen from grand rapids to places like waboden, who rely on lake winnipeg or the nelson river, are fed up with the debris released by hydro into the waters every year. with evident frustration, they show me photos of fish nets saturated with logs and willow bushes. the people at grand rapids want to cut out the brush in the spillway before it gets carried into the rivers and lakes. that's why they asked earlier in the summer what the plans were. they got the usual assurances from distracted bureaucrats. then they got a copy of an announcement made to the general public—no phone calls, no special acknowledgement. just a nameless fax. why bother caring about what a few aboriginal hunters or fishers think?

it was the last straw. newly elected chief mercredi, having taken the decision to return to his community rather than get on the consulting, board, academic, or government gravy train awaiting him, was not happy about the 5.5 million dollars hydro had given his community as compensation for the devastation caused by this 1960s project. mayor buck, in the midst of compensation negotiations, had been fighting for years to have hydro take his community's claims seriously, and was only too happy to join the new chief in the protest.

the grand rapids hydro project silenced a mighty river and harnessed its power in the 60s, when negotiations with first nations were not politically required or practised because the notion of aboriginal rights remained dormant. hydro built a beautiful suburban town for its own employees, and allowed the local hunters and fishermen to sink into a malaise. today a comparison of the hydro and aboriginal communities at grand rapids would be enough to belie anyone's sense that canada does not create its own race- and class-divided communities.

my former high-school classmate, gerald mckay, who sits on the town council, tells me the municipality has formally approved building a sign next to the "welcome to grand rapids"—the sign hydro sponsored. the new one will say: "welcome to ground zero. hydro profits near two billion dollars. compensation: zero." gerald also takes me to see ancient trails on the banks of the old riverbed, and the burial sites disturbed by the massive effort to build a dike for the project.

the paltry, belated compensation funds offered this first nation, and the paucity of imagination suffusing negotiations with the municipality, are manifestations of a public corporation that simply does not care about the indigenous people who live on the territories that produce its profits. the word "hydro" is a curse here, rarely used without other expletives attached. i amuse the locals by spitting every time i mention the utility.

i set up my tent, and spend the night with chief mercredi and mayor buck. the mayor, it turns out, plays guitar
and has a way with country tunes. the chief is quiet and
calm, showing an ease and determination that perhaps
come with having his feet on home ground. someone
brings robbie a large air mattress so he can sleep more
comfortably. throughout the next day, visitors come and
go. when i leave that evening there are at least 20 people—
families mostly—sitting in a large circle around the fire
with the two leaders.

when i return the next weekend, a full-fledged music
festival is gathering. about 80 people drop in and out that
evening, and all get their fill of moose-rib stew and cream
pie. the teens, who have been learning to play fiddle, show
their talents for an hour or so, and then a local master
fiddler and a few guitarists take over. soon some plywood
sheets are set up as a dance floor, and square dancing and
jigging get started. ovide takes evident pleasure in teaching some of the youngsters some jig steps and teasing the
older ladies about dancing with him. everyone harasses
mayor buck (he's just called "mayor") until he sings a
few songs.

it's spitting rain, but the generator keeps working—
the music is amplified, there are lights and we move in
and out from under the tarps as darkness settles around
the outer edges of the camp. something that deserves the

name "community" is re-enacted here; there's a warmth
and friendliness that passes among us. even the visiting
white folk are teased into dancing!

the suits show up
it appears that some of the decision makers have noticed
this event. bob brennan, president of manitoba hydro,
visits on september 15, 2004. he appears remorseful that
the corporation he's spent his life working for has such
a bad reputation. but apart from a few generalizations,
not much comes of the meeting, and the camp stays up.
premier gary doer travels up for a meeting at which the
larger issues are raised. it's the first time a sitting premier
has come up to grand rapids since the early 60s, when duff
roblin came to announce how much prosperity the dam
was going to bring.

elders charles osborne and gideon mckay, along with
jackson osborne and william osborne, from pimicikamak
cree nation—a community that has invented a range of
creative tactics in their own struggles with hydro—are
among the visitors from other communities. they come
to deliver a strong set of messages. they talk about many
things, but one powerful part of their message even crosses
the boundary of language: how a lone wolf gives a weak
howl, just loud enough to be heard by another. it re-
sponds, and slowly other wolves hear the call and respond,

and as their responses bounce back and forth they gather strength, until finally the power of the wolf nation is unmistakable.

in a small camp on a dry riverbed near the west shore of lake winnipeg, in the place where once great rapids with a healing power are now only a distant memory, the wolf has begun to howl. the camp was taken down shortly after a meeting with then premier doer that september. doer was apparently impressed and moved by the presentations he saw at grand rapids. a high-level consultation process has been established to examine the larger issues raised, though no new agreement appears to have as yet emerged from the discussions.

iii. how to build a legacy of hatred

northern manitoba, with some of the oldest "contact" history on the north american continent due to its central position in the english fur trade, has become over the last century a canadian backwater, rarely gaining attention even in alternative news sources. although a crucial struggle took place in the 70s over hydroelectric development, with the whole aboriginal community of south indian lake having to be relocated as a result of planned flooding, in general the conflict did not gain the media attention that was generated by the james bay cree or nwt dene. perhaps that is why manitoba hydro and the government of manitoba feel they can quietly get away with writing another page of colonial history on cree territory.

following the twists and turns of this conflict is not easy, but a bit of background is helpful. the community of nelson house signed treaty 5 in an adhesion, where first nations sign on to an existing treaty some years after it was negotiated, in 1908. since the treaty purported to surrender aboriginal land ownership, the cree of manitoba were not in a position to negotiate a modern treaty along the model of the james bay and northern québec agreement of 1975. in fact, in the mid 70s, manitoba hydro and its government partner thought they could do what they wanted without any aboriginal consent, and it was only determined opposition from five communities that led to a northern flood agreement in 1977. the nfa made some big promises; for example, as noted above, in a schedule attached to it the communities were promised "the eradication of mass poverty and mass unemployment." by a decade later, the government of manitoba and its publicly owned power utility decided the promises in the nfa were too big. they moved to negotiate what are misleadingly called "implementation agreements," effectively cash buyouts of the promises made in the nfa, in order to ensure that they were not legally liable for the promises they had made. to date, only one of the five communities, cross lake (centre of the pimicikamak cree nation), has courageously

refused the buyout and continues to lobby for real implementation of the nfa.

the community most effected by the 70s developments, south indian lake, did not have distinct band status. it was considered by government a "sub-community"
of nelson house and still, in 2004, did not have separate
band status, though citizens of south indian lake consider themselves a separate nation. it was not a separate
signatory of the nfa, though through some interesting
legal chicanery signed an implementation agreement itself
in the early 90s. among the stories that circulate in south
indian lake: people were paid to burn their houses in the
site of the old community to the ground. new houses
for the relocated community were built in southern
manitoba. during the move of those houses up north to
the new location of the community, insulation settled
in the walls, leaving a foot-long gap from the roof. the
houses were heated electrically, and the heat poured out
of the spaces. these "new" houses remain in use to this day.
small wonder some people in the community had their
power cut off for failing to pay the bills charged by the
company that flooded their lands and left them with in-
adequate housing…

although manitoba hydro assured everyone that the
environmental impacts of their projects would be minimal, and no environmental review was conducted, in fact

the projects had devastating effects. the churchill river was diverted so that it would flow into the nelson and add to the latter's rate of flow. this caused the effective destruction of a self-sustaining community at south indian lake for an aspect of the project that is only now really being used. so a whole community was condemned to fulfill some hydro planner's wet dreams! a dam (called jenpeg) was built near the south end of the nelson that effectively turned lake winnipeg into a giant water reservoir whose levels could be managed by engineers. the nelson river, once a pristine source of life, became silty and dangerous. at the time local people and independent engineers questioned the supposed neutral impact of the project; their objections were swept aside. i can remember seeing propaganda films in the early 70s boasting that the energy would have no negative environmental consequences. the hubris of manitoba hydro's engineers was trusted absolutely by a variety of manitoba governments, including the ndp government of ed schreyer. only after the project was complete was the impact clear. a generation of aboriginal leaders who had grown up going out on the land for emotional and material sustenance suddenly found their territory irreparably damaged: logs blocking access to the shore, undrinkable water, water levels that fluctuated according to no locally known logic making travel unsafe, interred bodies exposed, islands being slowly washed away.

hence, it is also small wonder that the first wave of hydro development created a legacy of distrust and even hatred for manitoba hydro on the part of many aboriginal peoples. the planners, engineers, and politicians had very little knowledge or respect for aboriginal culture, and saw treaty and aboriginal rights as inconveniences and obstacles to their "visionary" plans.

we are now seeing manitoba's own version of "phase 2," as a new premier and new corporate directors hear "the rustle of gold under their feet," to quote from a speech made by a chief during treaty 3 negotiations. the current plan is to develop three new dams, the first at wuskwatim near nelson house. knowing that public support for the plan will be easier to generate with a modicum of aboriginal consent, an agreement with the band council called *the summary of understandings between nisichawayasihk cree nation and manitoba hydro with respect to the wuskwatim project* was negotiated in october 2003. it should be noted that the current nelson house band council (part of the nisichawayasihk cree nation) came to office in a deeply divided election, in which their own elections appeals committee recommended re-holding the vote. the community operates under a "custom system" set up through the indian act: it is basically a community-determined electoral system with a constitution that, for example, provides for an election appeals committee. several individuals who were not eligible to run in the election for a variety of reasons in fact ran, thereby splitting some of the opposition votes. there were a series of other irregularities. the elected band council could rely on band funds to fight for its legitimacy, while its own appeals committee and those who wanted to contest the election had to use their own resources. eventually outside courts determined that the current council could continue to sit during the negotiations of wuskwatim, but its legitimacy was questioned by many in the community.

the deal itself is deeply flawed, especially when compared to the peace of the brave agreement negotiated in québec. the agreement basically involves a loan by manitoba hydro to nisichawayasihk cree nation so they can assume up to a one-third equity position in the project. that is, by assuming joint risk, they will become minority owners. they are not being compensated for developments taking place on their lands, or made into nation-to-nation partners in economic development, but rather being tossed a poisoned bone. the corporations being established to build and manage the project can meet without even having cree representatives present (quorum is a simple majority). although some changes were made to the design of the project at cree insistence, the language on environmental protection is quite weak (using the word "normally" to describe the parameters of water level movement). the *summary of understandings* (sou) is clearly not a treaty and not even binding. there are no standards in place to ensure fair process in the vote that must be held to ratify the final agreement that would ultimately flow from the sou. one academic, steven hoffman at the university of st. thomas in the united states, has said that "the agreement represents not the end of colonialism but its zenith."

at a january 2004 conference at the university of winnipeg, then minister of energy tim sale held up the wuskwatim project as a way of meeting kyoto accord targets, leading to cutbacks of coal emissions in the production of power in favour of "greener" hydroelectric power from northern manitoba. it would be good for the environment, good for the economy, good for everyone, according to the minister. try calling this a "greener" power source when you travel on the nelson river with local leaders and have to carry bottled water, as i did in the spring of 2003. there is no doubt southerners will experience benefits from the project, including less expensive power bills, less expensive power supplies for a variety of industries (private capital), and some capital accumulation by the manitoba state. the costs are all borne by northern aboriginal peoples, especially the hunters who rely on their ecological context to sustain an ancient way of life. but why bother caring about an ancient way of life? rights need only be applauded when they do not interfere with capital accumulation plans, with "progress" and "modernization" and "development."

at the clean environment commission hearings on the project, held in winnipeg and thompson, the commissioners heard some emotional testimony from the displaced residents of south indian lake, from the justice seekers of nelson house, and from a variety of individuals from the community and nation. the divisions between south indian lake and nelson house were clear, and the divisions within nelson house between a leadership determined to impose its new vision, which has gone so far as to pay community supporters a per diem to attend the hearings, and those from the community who at their own expense and some risk are determined to speak out against it. these speakers especially were concerned that their traditional hunting economy was once again being underestimated, that their northern homeland was again being seen as a colonial frontier (to slightly rewrite the terms of thomas berger's famous inquiry). why does manitoba feel it should give its aboriginal citizens less than québec appears to want to put on the table? have no lessons been learned by the northern manitoba debacle of the 70s?

in the end, after many delays, a vote was held on the project. the vote passed, but interestingly a few months before the vote the thousand potential "no" voters of south

indian lake were, after 20 years of trying, made into a separate band and thus ineligible to vote. it very likely would
have failed without that "small bit" of federal government
interference. almost as soon as construction began, a segment of the community began to express concerns about
lack of employment and the racial segmentation of the
dam work force. the dam ended up being constructed late
and with major cost overruns, and constructed at a time
when serious questions are being raised about whether
the power will be marketable. while premier selinger and
chief primrose posed proudly in 2012 for the papers, the
community continues to bear an unbearable load of social
problems, poverty, and misery beyond measure. "profits"
will only come to the community when the accountants at
manitoba hydro decide they have been made. which may
be many decades yet. if ever. and i wonder amidst all the
celebrations whether we have just built another legacy of
hatred in cree country.

iv. as long as the money flows...

it's a cold, freezing rain that's beating down on the tents
and tarps set up outside of the band office in tataskweyak
(formerly split lake) in spring 2012 when i make the first
of two short visits. the band office and nearby keeyask
negotiating office have been shut down, their fronts
"decorated" with a variety of handmade signs painted on

plywood sheets. among their slogans: "as long as the sun shines, grass grows and river flows," "no more lies," "we need a new chief," and "hobbs = rich, tcn = poor." a small camp of tarps, tents, and fires has been set up beside the band office: people who aren't willing to take it anymore are determined to keep the band office shut until something is done.

the community itself, placed in a jewel of a northern bush setting, surrounded by water, is in obviously grim shape—so many boarded up and burned-out houses—the whole place with a gulag-like feel. a teacher i chat with at the fire talks of the difficulty of teaching in classrooms where mice are ever-present and where children are playing with mice droppings. i see houses built on foundations of plywood. at least five houses, i've been told by albertine spence (a social worker), have been found to be contaminated with e. coli. if this was white southern ontario it would be a national scandal. but it's cree northern manitoba so no one gives a damn.

well, manitoba hydro gives a dam (or, at least, gets a dam). this community was promised prosperity when the first hydro dams were built nearby, especially the giant limestone dam in the 70s. the nfa would end their problems. then they were promised prosperity when they signed an implementation agreement in 1992: the money would solve their problems. they are being promised even more prosperity as the coming keeyask and conawapa dams slowly work their way from the ever-growing hubris of manitoba's engineers to their drafting tables. too much more of this kind of "prosperity" and the whole community can become a poster child for the word "misery." perhaps it already is.

the demands of the protesters have long been a staple of those local people with enough determination, hope, and energy to try to wade through the labyrinthine maze of structures and agencies and corporations and, well, dissimulation and bad faith that have been like a plague over the past 10 years or longer. basically, more than anything, they want some of the high-flying manitoba hydro players to start addressing the immediate and urgent social problems. but this won't happen, they feel, until the consulting companies and lawyers playing a major role in the community are removed. and that won't happen until there are changes among the local leadership. so, three interrelated demands that come from a grassroots movement. let's look at each one a bit more closely.

it's been known for a while now that millions of dollars are flowing into the community from manitoba hydro to support the development of the keeyask dam. a partnership agreement was approved by the community in the last few years, adding to the northern flood agreement (1976), implementation agreement (1992), and various amendments to the latter signed in the last 10 years (at least two). the community has set up a variety of corporations, bypassing the community controlled development corporation set up two decades ago when the implementation agreement was signed with hydro. this new set of corporations is not community-controlled and is only very indirectly responsible to the community. the same few individuals sit on its board, are paid per diems for its meetings (and any other meetings on hydro-related matters), and make the decisions. so the paradox is that there is real and desperate poverty for most, and a lot of money flowing to a few. the federal government is currently looking at putting the band into receivership, while its high flyers and their ever-present consultant "friends" boast in public meetings in the south of being from a "progressive and prosperous" community. it is the acuteness of the social misery, the discovery of e. coli in the middle of an existing housing crisis, while the band has been so poorly run that its federal core finances are massively in the red, that finally led people here to say enough is enough.

and, by the way, one thing the hard-nosed tough negotiating company doesn't like people in the community to know is that when the community signed its adhesion to treaty 5, long ago, the chief was handed the wrong piece of paper. that mistake was never corrected. to this date the federal government does not have a surrender document from tataskweyak that gives them "certainty" over lands: aboriginal title remains vested in the community. tataskweyak, it turns out, was always in the position of the james bay cree, with unsurrendered aboriginal title as a strong negotiating lever. but to say so would upset their cozy relationship with manitoba hydro, so consultants and lawyers doing such "tough" negotiations studiously look the other way.

one of the issues at the forefront in the spring of 2012 was how much time the "local" leadership spent outside of the community. part of how individuals like this get elected stems from the flawed corbiere decision at the supreme court of canada in 1999, which allowed off-reserve members to vote and run for office in first nations. this means people without a necessary attachment or interest in what happens on the ground in their first nation because they commonly live in distant urban centres may be inclined to vote for individuals whose only concern is for what they can financially gain. hence, for much of the time chief and councillors rarely attended community meetings. they jumped, and high, when hydro or its consultant asked them for a meeting in winnipeg, however. they ran from town when they discovered that conditions had reached a new low: when e. coli was found in the water of five houses the reaction of the then leadership was to leave town for more meetings with hydro, as quickly as they could. there was an election in the fall of 2012, and with it hope for a more community-based, engaged leadership that would not kowtow to the vulture consultants that long held an iron grip on the community.

the final demand is that a winnipeg-based consulting company called hobbes and associates, which has worked for the community for more than a decade negotiating the keeyask agreement, is removed from its position. interestingly, the first nation's law firm also works for the consultant, putting it into a conflict of interest should the community decide to part ways with the consultant. when a former chief, emile garson, tried to get rid of the consulting company, the lawyers wrote a band council resolution for the rest of the councillors to sign, effectively sidelining that chief. fast forward to spring 2012: when a majority of band councillors signed a resolution removing the consultant and sidelining the pro-consultant chief, the same lawyers worked with that chief to sidestep the council. it is clear to me that outsiders are playing for their own interest over that of their clients, but making for a nice and cozy relationship with each other as long as the money flows. the consulting company has not worked itself out of a job by training local people to take over for it. we wonder how hard or effectively they negotiate with a utility that antes up the cash to a "neutral" third party.

the utility wants negotiations to follow a certain model: the partnership model they used on the wuskwatim project. the utility doesn't like québec's peace of the brave agreement. so the supposedly "tough" negotiators of the consulting company negotiate a partnership agreement and band councillors, when asked, haven't heard of resource revenue sharing or the peace of the brave. that is, local leaders are not being made aware that other models and other options exist. and the lawyers and consultants get quite the cheques: over the last 15 years, it appears that about 100 million dollars has been paid to the community to negotiate the new hydro projects. the amount will be deducted from the final settlement, no doubt, so it doesn't cost hydro anything. it is "only" a part of the community's future. by the calculation of community members, about two-thirds of that money or 66 million dollars has gone directly to the consulting company, lawyers, and other outside technical experts. they sure have nice christmas parties.

there are issues here—corruption, poverty, deal making—that involve basic human rights and the dignity of people. at this level of politics, when faced with these levels of social trauma, one is inclined to discard the layers of theory and just ask for a measure of fairness. but aboriginal and treaty rights are intimately bound up with this struggle in a way that cannot be so easily disentangled. if the aboriginal title that was not surrendered by the treaty were being respected, if someone in the morass of negotiations had real respect for the value of aboriginal rights and the concomitant value of traditional indigenous knowledge, then a path out of this morass, not based on a fickle humanist compassion but rather founded on a clear, legally established entitlement, could be broached.

instead, a community in dire misery is subsidizing extra swimming pools for a pack of lawyers, consultants, engineers, and administrators; a few community members live high off the hog on permanent per diems. this is a scandal. i challenge the lawyers, the consultants, manitoba hydro's executives and board members, to do as i did and spend a few nights in the house of someone from tataskw-eyak. look around. then tell me with a straight face about the "prosperity" they've brought the community. and tell my daughter, who met a blind girl younger than her 11 years, who was homeless and for whom the school had no braille supports. remind that girl how prosperous she is because she might be inclined to forget. the treaty prom-ises were supposed to last as long as the sun shines, the grasses grow, and the rivers run. and this community did not, as it happens, surrender its aboriginal title through treaty. it appears that so many brilliant minds planning ta-taskweyak's future won't care as long as the money flows… to them!

v. marginal comment on another new building in downtown winnipeg

in the old days the army would walk back into the city in a grand parade, carrying and displaying the spoils of war in a triumphal procession. these days they just build new buildings. a few years ago the ribbon was cut to open a new downtown headquarters for manitoba hydro. everyone was there, and they were all shaking hands. and smiling. you think: "maybe it will help to rejuvenate winnipeg's downtown!" you think: "they made it using the ecologically latest features and materials!" (though you have some dim memory that recycling existing buildings is the most ecologically friendly architectural practice.) you think: "maybe it'll be beautiful?!" but you really doubt it. even if it is or especially if it is "beautiful," what does this triumphal monument say to the people whose lands have been flooded and rivers degraded, whose difficult lives are stories of overcoming or surrendering to the odds stacked against them by people in suits in boardrooms? as the greedy powerful and their devoted hirelings smile and shake hands and shake hands smiling and shaking shaking and smiling and you think: "if the tears don't fall now, when will they ever fall?"

postscript: bush culture for a bush country: an unfinished manifesto

the bush is calling to some of us. it invites us to add, multiply, and supplement its signs and texts; to write straight off the trail that is written through it; to continue that trace that meanders and guides some of us through its multiplicities, its polymorphic playfulness, its multivoicedness; and, of course, to leave that track and create others: a coming community? perhaps. something unnamed that is in and of the bush.

the bush can be deployed as an allegory for something some of us desire, something some of us, those who carry western culture with us every step of the way, can almost touch but never quite reach. when many of us are in the bush, we bring with us that which is not bush. so we travel uneasily through it. the bush designates that vast part of the country that remains outside of the strip malls, covered for the most part in rock, swamp, and water, though some of it is tundra and some of it is mountain and some of it is prairie. a bush culture is a culture that is of the bush. and bush, unlike wilderness, allows us to think a lived relation to and in this landscape. first nations cultures, in my view, are bush cultures. the most important fracture line in canadian culture is not and has never been the linguistic one that separates franco- from anglo-. the most important cultural fracture line has been the division between aboriginal and non-aboriginal, and the conversations that cross this boundary. many other differences, literally, pale in comparison. but some part of canadian culture, that non-existent that pretends to claim "us" all, is also of the bush. if we can have the bush, if we can have our bush leagues, our bush doctors, our bush texts, our bush bikes, our bush women and bush men, our bush pilots, our bush whackers, our bush radios, our bush camps, we might as well imagine what it would be to have a bush country.

i was once asked, enjoined, to think the unthinkable (which is actually *an* rather than *the* unthinkable, which is actually a thinkable unthinkable): canada without québec. canada without québec: what will happen, what will remain? what will happen, of course, can be specified with acute philosophical precision: nothing. nothing will happen when québec leaves. we will barely awaken the morning after to sleepwalk our way through other days.

those of us who are the fortunate and privileged will go to our workplaces, drive or ride along the same familiar roads, sit in the same offices, read the same newspapers. the sky will sit firmly in its position. nothing will have happened. those who are not fortunate and privileged will continue, as before, to struggle to survive and to change society. canada is and will be that great postmodern nation for this precise reason: nothing ever happens here. that's why some of us love it. at least, let this be the shield under which we protect our subversive activities from the normalizing gaze of the imperial power we border.

some calculators will undoubtedly be at work in some other offices, and these will have some long-term material effects. interest rates will rise, one speculates, bond ratings will lower, firmer voices in favour of government deficit cutting will emerge in all their masculine strength to deploy their codes of discipline and restraint. and these things, which seem to go ahead regardless of québec, will continue to be barely noticeable, except to those who are thrown from their jobs, houses, lives, as the cost that never makes it into the formulas of the calculators.

what will remain? this is the question of moment. again, what will remain is sadly far too predictable. canada will remain canada. not english canada nor english-speaking canada—a designation that has never had much accuracy—since at least in nunavut and denendeh questions of language will remain acute. nor t.r.o.c., the rest of canada, a delightful acronym that only serves to centre québec at the expense of some of us and identifies some of us through our wounds. what will remain is canada; canada will remain canada. what this canada designates will be a matter of borders and of justice.

others want to desire canada because it embodies enlightenment principles in its liberal and democratic institutions, in its creation of a public space that is "accessible" and "open." but to descendants of the earliest canadians, aboriginal peoples, those same liberal democratic institutions are totalizing and have become totalitarian. to a select, privileged few, the existing institutions are just; and why not, since those institutions serve the needs of those few. the first nations, however, are not well served by these principles and these institutions. the value of the debate over québec is that it opens a space of questioning, a space of questioning that allows some of us to imagine centring what has previously been marginal, of overturning hierarchies, of imagining a canada, with or without québec, that embodies in its borderings, some vision of justice: imagining bush country.

borders

in a sojourn outside of canada, in a united state, i was asked frequently about "the québec question" by my american comrades. "where will all this lead?" they asked. my reply was "to tanks on the 401." notwithstanding the obvious truth of my contention that canada defines a social reality where nothing happens, this possibility remains. there are other places in the world where it was assumed that "it can never happen here"; and in part this willed blindness has led to it happening. the "it" being civil war. we already have a rhetoric of civil war, a rhetorical civil war, the threat of threats, angry gestures, posturings and plan b's. so it must be said here, now, and again there, then: québec must permit itself and be allowed to leave peacefully should they decide they want to go. by engaging in an act of peaceful separation, in that alone, canada can be true to its best bush spirit and offer a worthwhile spectacle for contemplation by historians and the rest of the world. those of us who return to the bush must insistently remind those who escalate the rhetoric that peace—one of our constitutional foundations after all—must ultimately and immediately be actively constructed. in this situation it can no longer be assumed. in all our debates and dialogues let some of us remember to call for peace.

with or without québec—this phrase will override all the deliberations of this unfinished manifesto, because the presence or absence of québec has no bearing on the notion of justice that some of us subscribe to, the question of québec merely allows an opening to the question of justice—canada must, now, fulfill its ethical obligations to its aboriginal people. of course, this issue is of great moment in the québec debate. québecois treatment of aboriginal peoples, it is sometimes said outside québec, is a great cause for concern. the québecois have shown little regard for aboriginal rights; can we allow them to separate under these conditions? all this concern circulating as if "we" in this instance occupied some kind of moral high ground. from the perspective of a bush culture there is no difference: both in québec and outside it, aboriginal rights are due a respect they have not been given. so let there be no hypocrisy on this point. yes, aboriginal rights here and now. yes, aboriginal rights there and now. the call is not "québec cannot separate because it has no program of justice for first nations," but rather the call must insist that the same logic that entitles québec to separate entitles the first nations of québec and the first nations outside of québec to at least the same level of self-determination.

two borders remain meaningful. the border between canada and the states that remain united to our south. and the border between bush culture and mall culture. the call for borders is never an appealing call; borders have no place in the bush. however, some of us must work with what we are given, and in this world the border that marks a difference with our neighbours to the south is that which we have been given. at a bare minimum, at the zero degree of nationhood, canada makes sense inasmuch as it is not a united state. in the world today resistance to global hegemony, to dominating power, means precisely staying outside of the united states' sphere of influence. hence, our border, inasmuch as we have to have a border, can be made and to some extent already marks that we are not them. it is of no use to us though, if we go through the bother of having that border and then capitulate at every turn culturally.

the second border marks this struggle. there is a lived border that separates something called the canadian north from its south. the south designates that lived reality that is experienced by most of the population of canada, who live within a single hundred miles of their imperial southern neighbours. that reality, whether english- or french-speaking, is depressingly similar—embodies and carries forward—to life in a united state. it's not so much a matter of the same television programs being watched, as the same modality of watching television taking place. this is mall culture, the strip mall view that defines contemporary civilization, a civilization that is hurtling toward its teleological pinnacle. on this level, there is no significant difference between minnesotans and manitobans, between québecois and cajun, between a haitian immigrant struggling to cope in washington and a haitian immigrant struggling to cope in montreal.

elsewhere, north of this border, there remains another possibility. bush women, bush men still exist and engage a mode of social being that enters the bush, that is of the bush, that is not civilized, that does not belong in shopping malls, that is not seen on television, that is not spoken in parliamentary debate. what are its operating principles, apart from the fact that burping and farting are not restricted, that the body remains in force? at a minimal level, a bush culture involves an ethic of speech. not a freedom of speech that remains sacrosanct to the exact degree that nothing important can be enunciated. but a freedom to listen, a speech that is responsible, that circulates around some notion of respect. a bush culture does not involve an end to repression, a universal abandon, a forsaking of law and rule, but a different modality of law and rule, a different order of repression, even.

north, like the bush, designates in this context an epistemological direction rather than a spatial one. there are malls in the north. more and more of them, and more televisions, too. this is called progress, where from the perspective of the bush it is precisely imperialism, whether being carried on by franco or anglo canadians. in the north we can see this border more clearly in the difference between a place like old crow, or colville lake, or pond inlet, on the one hand, and prince george, or norman wells, or nanisivik, on the other. it's a matter of trajectory, embodied in urban design and architecture and attitude. one place relies on and opens up to the bush, the other defends itself from and huddles uneasily against its landscape. in both places, you can still look a stranger in the eye and get a smile in response to your own: but in the latter those smiles are disappearing fast.

there is also bush in our largest urban centres. this is harder to find, a border more felt and cultural than pointed to. there are friendship centres, and cultural gatherings of people who have come from far away, where children are allowed to make their presence known. there are all those who do not belong in the shopping malls, but still, for some reason, find themselves there. there are nomads on the streets. there is wildness in the alleyways. there are crack wars. it's not always pleasant: those who would paper over the pain are perhaps marginally more ethical than those who revel in reproducing the discourse of despair. scattered here and there in the cities we can even find a subversive architecture that draws its inspiration from the bush: the mobile homes of the very poor or the canadian shield-like forms of the paradoxically named museum of civilization or the vernacular play of old town in yellowknife. a person who relates to a building not as the site of meetings or a capital investment or a status symbol, but a warm air duct that promises the possibility of sleep, is living the city as bush.

a bush culture looks to the cities as much as to forest and tundra. where did the punks get their mohawks from? people sometimes travel over the most far-flung corners of bush country, hunting from the air, carrying with them the full force of their masculine codes of civilization. others, cast off at the bottom of the skyscrapers, remember to pay their respects, embodying still and against all odds the order of the bush.

so, let some of us redraw the borders. let us attempt to draw a border and hive off the north, mark out the bush, give it geographical respectability. at least we could do one pragmatic thing that would actually be of use to the country, and create a province out of the so-called mid north. let attawapiskat and shamattawa and sheshatshit, or kenora and thompson and goose bay, have their commonality and the imperial centres to the south have theirs. let the maps acknowledge the colonial reality, though they could never spatially represent the epistemic reality.

justice

there can be no justice in canada without some adequate recognition of the calls of its first nations. remaining buried in the history of canada, the injustices upon which the nation is historically and philosophically founded have returned like some freudian repressed moment to dirty the edges of our more sterile discussions of the québec question. whether or not québec goes away, these injustices will not. they will not simply disappear. they will remain to trouble some of us. others do seem to have succeeded at forgetting they have a conscience, and carry forward the strip malling of the country with an unenviable industry; they are the worker drones of totalizing culture. we find them in the highest offices of the nation, and in the elite pantheon of the culture industry. but the injustices remain, and no amount of pavement will cover them over. a just country cannot found itself on injustice: there can never be justice without justice.

all the ghosts in this country are in the bush, where the killing took place. the spirits of the country are in the bush, roaming restlessly through the dreams of those whose bodies are marked with the trace of history forced on them, the history that hurts, the history that is not a story of how every day in every way things got better and better. these ghosts haunt the québec bush as surely as they haunt the ontario bush. the earliest québecois, at least, coureurs de bois, went into the bush and some, many, were inspired enough to embrace it. the earliest english perched precariously and suspiciously on its edges; but they, at least, in some stunted form, were willing to acknowledge its otherness and enshrine some notion of aboriginal rights. the spirits remain in the bush. and the spirit of the country is its bush. this must not become some paved-over cultural claim that allows concrete bush scenes to be sculpted into bay street buildings: it has to be a claim with a trajectory that rubs against the grain, that in the resistances it provokes reminds us of the civilized brutality of the power that seeks to harness and eradicate it. so here is a minimum program of this manifesto: let's recognize that more first nations have more power over more land. every step in this direction will be in accord with the spirit of the bush, will move on the trajectory of a bush culture, of a respect for aboriginal and treaty rights.

it is instructive to remember that institutional multi-culturalism, a grand canadian cultural and political project, was itself a totalizing device deployed by a liberal government to elide the specific, particular claims of two social groups whose call was not for a universal, undifferentiated equality but rather for recognition: québec and the variety of first nations. in this form, multiculturalism says, offers the injunction, "celebrate cultural difference" in the same tone as "put on a happy face," the intensity of the command necessarily in inverse proportion to the misery that has to be overcome. by doing so the official multicultural project hides the fact that some cultures qualitatively differ from others, some differences are more different than others. there are multiculturalisms that are capable of recognizing this.

curiously, in moving towards a recognition of first nations and aboriginal rights, our discourse itself undergoes

a shift. other possibilities emerge. in fact, principles of social justice and of democracy are embodied in the substantive features of first nations societies. when we look to the
bush, we begin by looking to the people of the bush. here
we find the most interesting, complex, engaged, sublime,
dramatic, vital, thought-provoking, intensely charged cultural productions of the country; of the rest, very little—
and that by far the best—is not an echo of some other
ethos, following an impulse to imitate. therefore it can
be said that by being just, it is possible to find justice. the
blindness and refusals of some are not merely—though it
would be bad enough—unjust in and of themselves. these
blindnesses and refusals structure into speech a refusal of
justice, they repress, deny, constrain their own history. this
is solid foundation for a shopping mall. it will not do for
a country.

what will do, for this country at least, is a look into
the bush, a few steps away from civilization, a rethinking
that places special value on meaningful difference. the difference between how peter mansbridge and lisa laflamme
read the news, disseminate information, is nearly trivial.
the difference between how peter mansbridge and an-
gela sidney tell a story is a matter of an entirely different
register. the bush is a space of qualitative difference, the
feel of sitting on this rock overlooking this beaver dam,
rather than that rock and that pond. a palimpsest space

overwritten by glaciers and beavers and berry pickers and winds and satellites and partridges and lightning-lit fires and nomadic hunters and dramatic storms and the shrieking of crows against high winds. try to paint it, try to see it: a more difficult proposition than it sounds. the bush is a great site for play and for possibility; for repetition and for difference. you can find the bush, even in the eaton centre, but first you have to get the mall out of your head.

.the problem of québec is that until recently the question was deeply boring. whether or not to establish another liberal (read, bourgeois) democracy in the northern part of the americas. ho hum. the energies of young people fighting for their right to a future as i adapt these words, in 2012, causes me pause though: something exciting is happening there: a future has yet to be written. it is possible, though, to have much as much or even more fun than that here, in this country, where nothing ever happens. paradoxically, that fun can be had while engaging in the highest ethical call for responsibility. it is possible to have a bush culture for a bush country.

sources

alfred, taiaiake. *wasase*. peterborough: broadview press, 2005.

arendt, hannah. *the origins of totalitarianism*. new york: harcourt brace jovanovich, 1973.

asch, michael. *home and native land*. toronto: methuen, 1983.

___ . ed. *aboriginal and treaty rights in canada*. vancouver: university of british columbia press, 1997.

brody, hugh. *the other side of eden: hunters, farmers and the shaping of the world*. vancouver: douglas and mcintyre, 2001.

___ . *living arctic*. vancouver: douglas and mcintyre, 1987.

chodkiewicz, jean luc and jennifer brown. eds. *first nations and hydroelectric development in northern manitoba*. winnipeg: the centre for rupertsland studies, 1999.

cumming, peter a. and neil mickenberg. *native rights in canada*. toronto: the general press, 1973.

hall, anthony. *the american empire and the fourth world*. montreal: mcgill-queen's university press, 2003.

hawthorne, h.b. *a survey of the contemporary indians of canada: economic, political, educational needs and policies*. 2 vols. ottawa: queen's printer, 1966-67.

henderson, james youngblood. *first nations jurisprudence and aborigi-nal rights: defining the just society.* saskatoon: native law centre, 2006.

kulchyski, peter. *like the sound of a drum: aboriginal cultural politics in denendeh and nunavut.* winnipeg: univerity of manitoba press, 2005.

___. ed. *unjust relations: aboriginal rights in canadian courts.* toronto: oxford university press, 1994.

marx, karl. *capital.* volume one. trans. ben fowkes. new york: vintage books, 1977.

marx, karl and friedrich engels. *proceedings of the sixth rhine province assembly. third article. debates on the law on thefts of wood.* trans. clemens duttin. in *karl marx frederick engels: collected works.* vol. 1. eds. n. karamanova, m. lopukhina, v. schnittke, and l. zubrilova. new york: international publishers, 1975. 224-63.

milloy, john. *a national crime: the canadian government and the resi-dential school system.* winnipeg: university of manitoba press, 1999.

monture-angus, patricia. *journeying forward: dreaming first nations' independence.* halifax: fernwood, 2003.

morris, alexander. *the treaties of canada with the indians of manitoba and the north west territories including the negotiations on which they were based, and other information relating thereto.* saskatoon: fifth house publishers, 1991.

neve, alex. speech. the university of regina, september 2009. revised and published as "canada and the un declaration on the rights of indigenous peoples: opposition must give way to implementa-tion." alex neve and craig benjamin. *prairie forum* 36 (fall 2011): 1-8.

richardson, boyce. *strangers devour the land.* new york: knopf, 1975.

ross, rupert. *returning to the teachings: exploring aboriginal justice.* toronto: penguin books, 1996.

spivak, gayatri chakravorty. *a critique of post colonial reason.* cambridge: harvard university press, 1999.

supreme court of canada. *r v drybones* (1969) scr 282.

supreme court of canada. *attorney general of canada v lavell/ isaac v bedard* (1974) scr 1349.

supreme court of canada. *calder v attorney general of british columbia* (1973) scr 313.

supreme court of canada. *guerin v the queen* (1984) 2 scr 335.

supreme court of canada. *r. v sparrow* (1990) 1 scr 1075.

supreme court of canada. *r. v sioui* (1990) 1 scr 1025.

supreme court of canada. *r v van der peet* (1996) 2 scr 507.

supreme court of canada. *corbiere v canada* (1999) 2 scr 203.

taylor, diana. *the archive and the repertoire.* durham: duke university press, 2003.

thompson, e.p. *customs in common.* new york: the new press, 1993.

watkins, mel. ed. *dene nation.* toronto: university of toronto press, 1978.

wenzel, george w. *animal rights, human rights: ecology, economy, and ideology in the canadian arctic.* university of toronto press, 1991.

wolf, eric r. *europe and the people without history.* berkeley: university of california press, 1982.